GRE Vocab

Capacity

2022 Edition

**Powerful Memory Tricks and Mnemonics
to Learn GRE Vocabulary Words**

Now with more than 1,300 mnemonics!

By

Brian McElroy

and

Vince Kotchian

Contents

Why This Book Is Different

There are tons of books, apps, and websites designed to help you learn GRE words. However, if you've tried typical vocabulary study methods, they might not have worked very well for you.

The problem with most vocabulary products is that the sentences in the books are boring! Your brain might not naturally form connections to the meanings of words if they're not presented to you in a memorable, creative way.

GRE Vocab Capacity is different. We've not only clearly defined the words but we've also created sentences designed to help you remember the words through a variety of unusual associations - using **mnemonics**.

Mnemonic Examples

A mnemonic is just a memory device. It works by creating a link in your brain to something else, so that recall of one thing helps recall of the other. This can be done in many ways – but the strongest links are through senses, emotions, rhymes, and patterns.

Consider this example:

> **quash** (verb): to completely stop from happening.
>
> Think: **squash.**
>
> The best way to **quash** an invasion of ants in your kitchen is simple: **squash** them.

Now your brain has a link from the word **quash** (which it may not have known) to the word **squash** (which it probably knows). Both words sound and look the same, so it's easy to create a visual and aural link. If you picture someone squashing ants (and maybe get grossed out), you have another visual link as well as an emotional link.

Here's another example:

> **eschew** (verb): to avoid.
>
> Think: **ah-choo!**
>
> **Eschew** people who say "**ah-choo!**" unless you want to catch their colds.

The word **eschew** sounds similar to a sneeze (**ah-choo!**), so your brain will now link the two sounds. If you picture yourself avoiding someone who is about to sneeze in your face, even better! Again, the more connections you make in your brain to the new word, the easier it will be for you to recall it.

Word Root Examples

Word roots are parts of words that often mean the same thing. For example, the root **chron** pretty much always has something to do with time: syn**chron**ize, **chron**ological, etc. So knowing what word roots mean can be useful in helping you learn words. They can also provide a hint for the meaning of words that you don't know.

However, English is a funny language, and roots don't always have the same meaning - it can depend on what word they're in. So what you *shouldn't* expect from roots is that they'll be reliable to help you determine the definition of a word you don't know. Keep in mind that knowing your word roots is not a substitute for knowing the actual definitions of words.

We've included an appendix with this book that lists many common word roots along with their usual definitions, and an easy example word that uses the root. For example:

chron: time.

Think: **chron**ological: arranged in order of time.

We recommend learning all the word roots if you have time. It may be helpful to learn all the word roots first and then begin learning words you don't know, looking for instances of the roots to help you learn the new words.

Word Root Tip: the more letters you can match from the beginning of a word you do know to a word you don't know, the more likely it is they have similar meanings. Matching five or more letters is a good benchmark.

For example, if you know that **pacifist** has to do with being peaceful, you'd be right in guessing that **pacific** has a similar meaning since they both start with **pacifi**.

How To Use This Book

One tool we recommend is periodic review of flashcards. The "tactile learning" (in other words, learning by doing) aspect of making your own cards is very effective. Buying pre-made flashcards skips this step, and you miss out on an opportunity to "write it down in your head" by physically writing the words and definitions down yourself.

Here's an example of what a flashcard might look like:

prodigal

(prah-dig-ul)

---

prodigal (adjective): wasteful

Think: **Prada gal**.

The **prodigal Prada gal** spent $1900 on a pair of boots.

syn: spendthrift, profligate

Notice that the front of the card just has the word with its pronunciation. Using the word when talking to someone that day will help you learn it.

The back of the card contains a brief definition, a mnemonic (which you can invent or find in this book), a sentence using the word in a way that calls to mind its meaning, and any synonyms of the word you'd also like to learn (try an online dictionary like m-w.com to look up synonyms of a word).

Here's a method and chart that describe the order with which to study your cards:

1) Create 50 custom vocabulary flashcards:

   a) Side A shows the word and its pronunciation.

   b) Side B shows the definition, part-of-speech, mnemonic, sample sentence, and synonym(s).

2) Label the cards with numbers 1-50 and stack them in order.

3) Use the table below to decide which cards to study and review each day.

GRE Vocab Capacity – 2022 Edition

DAY	STUDY	REVIEW	REVIEW AGAIN
1	Cards 1-5		
2	Cards 6-10		
3	Cards 11-15		
4	Cards 16-20	Cards 1-5	
5	Cards 21-25	Cards 6-10	
6	Cards 26-30	Cards 11-15	
7	Cards 31-35	Cards 16-20	
8	Cards 36-40	Cards 21-25	
9	Cards 41-45	Cards 26-30	
10	Cards 46-50	Cards 31-35	
11		Cards 36-40	Cards 1-5
12		Cards 41-45	Cards 6-10
13		Cards 46-50	Cards 11-15
14			Cards 16-20
15			Cards 21-25
16			Cards 26-30
17			Cards 31-35
18			Cards 36-40
19			Cards 41-45
20			Cards 46-50
21	REVIEW ALL 50 CARDS Separate out any cards you haven't mastered yet into a new pile, and add new cards to this pile until you have 50 cards again that you don't know.		

Other Learning Tips

For troublesome words - or for any word you want to be sure of - we recommend writing down the word's definition *in your own words*, then making up your own sentence using the word. Until you can explain something in your own words, you probably don't fully understand it, and your own definitions and sentences will often be more memorable than ours.

Some people go straight to the most bizarre looking words in the book, but don't overlook the words that you "kind of" know but can't easily define. That goes for words outside this book, too. If you can't easily define a word you see in the newspaper, for instance, look it up! The context you read it in will help you learn it.

For words that just won't stick in your brain, try associating a movement with the word. Making a specific gesture with your body every time you study the word will provide an additional connection in your memory.

A few more suggestions:

Modify it. If you don't like our mnemonic or think that it can be improved, then use your own. They are your own customized cards to do with what you like. Even draw a picture or make a collage if it helps.

Shuffle. When studying a group of cards, don't always study them in the same order, so your brain won't be able to associate one card with another.

Study before bed. Studies have shown that memorization-type tasks are best studied during the hours preceding a full night's sleep. One popular theory to explain this phenomenon is that when we sleep, our mind organizes the day's events, starting with the most recent ones.

One last tip: **use it or lose it**! The more you can work your new vocabulary into your daily speech and writing, the more you'll remember it. You might sound nerdy, but it's worth it.

Our hope is that this book not only helps you improve your vocabulary, but also inspires you to start creating your own mnemonics!

– Brian and Vince

P.S. - We encourage you to write a review of *GRE Vocab Capacity* on Amazon.com to tell others about your experience with the book.

Please contact us directly for suggestions that you might have so we can improve the book for future readers.

We're also available for private tutoring of the GRE, as well as the GMAT, SAT, ACT, and ISEE - either in person (in San Diego) or online (via Skype).

mcelroy@post.harvard.edu (Brian McElroy)

vince@vincekotchian.com (Vince Kotchian)

www.McElroyTutoring.com or vincekotchian.com

The Mnemonics

abase (verb): to humiliate or degrade. "uh BASE"

Think: give up **a base**.

When you're making out with someone, if you give up **a base** too quickly, then you just **abase** yourself.

abashed (adjective): embarrassed. "uh BASHED"

Think: **Bashful** the dwarf.

When Snow White kisses him, **Bashful** gets so **abashed** that he blushes.

abate (verb): to reduce. "uh BATE"

Think: **rebate**.

It may be annoying to have to mail it in, but the **rebate** on the new cell phone will **abate** its cost.

aberration (noun): an exception or departure from the norm. "ah (rhymes with "nah") burr A shun"

Think: **a bare Asian**.

Seeing **a bare Asian** would be an **aberration** – most people in Asia wear clothes.

abeyance (noun): temporary inactivity; suspension. "uh BAY ants"

Think: **"obey" ends**.

When our lieutenant's command to **obey ends**, our work plans are held in **abeyance** because we're lazy.

abhor (verb): to hate. "ab WHORE"

Think: **ab-whore**.

Daria **abhors** the tube-top-wearing blonde who stole her boyfriend and refers to her as an "**ab-whore**".

abject (adjective): miserable; wretched. "ab-JEKT"

Think: **rejects**.

If she **rejects** my marriage proposal, I'll be **abject**, with nothing to live for.

abnegate (verb): to give up something; to deny oneself something. "ab nuh GATE"

Think: **abs negated.**

If you **abnegate** food, the fat covering your **abs** will get **negated**.

abomination (noun): something awful.
"uh BOM in A shun"

Think: **bomb a nation.**

It is an **abomination** to **bomb a nation**: civilians get killed.

aboriginal (adjective): existing since the beginning.
"AB or IDGE in ul"

Think: **original.**

In Australia, the **original** natives are the Aborigines - they are **aboriginal** since they were its first inhabitants.

abort (verb): to end prematurely. "uh BORT"

Think: **abortion.**

An **abortion** can **abort** a pregnancy.

abound (verb): to be numerous. "uh BOUND"

Think: **abundant**.

Kangaroos **abound** in Australia; they're **abundant**, bouncing around wherever you look.

abrasive (adjective): causing irritation. "Uh BRAY sive"

Think: **braying donkey.**

Adopting a homeless **donkey** seemed great until I realized it would wake me up every morning with its **abrasive braying.**

abridge (verb): to shorten. "uh BRIJ"

Think: **a bridge**.

A **bridge** would **abridge** my commute, which involves driving around the canyon.

abrogate (verb): to get rid of; to abolish. "AB roh gate"

Think: **a broken gate.**

After my 120 lb. Mastiff decided to **abrogate** the barrier to the kitchen and eat from the garbage, we were left with **a broken gate.**

abscission (noun): the shedding of leaves, flowers, or fruits. "ab SIZH un"

Think: **scissors**.

Instead of waiting for the grapes to drop off of the vines, speed up the **abscission** by getting out there with a pair of **scissors**.

absolute (adjective) complete and total. "ab so LUTE"

Think: **Absolut Vodka.**

The reason **Absolut Vodka** is more expensive than most brands is its superior purity; it is literally **absolute** vodka.

absolve (verb): to free from guilt; to forgive. "ub SOLVE"

Think: **dissolve**.

Catholics believe that confessing to a priest will **dissolve** their guilt and **absolve** them from sin.

abstemious (adjective): sparing; moderate.
"ab STEM ee us"

Think: **abstinence**.

The health teacher knew that if he told students to be **abstemious**, some of them would still get pregnant, so he urged them to practice **abstinence**.

abstruse (adjective): hard to comprehend. "ab STROOS"

Think: **abstract** and **confusing**.

The **abstract** strudel directions will **confuse** the new cook because they are **abstruse**.

abysmal (adjective): awful. "uh BIZ mull"

Think: **Pepto-Bismol**.

When I had food poisoning, my stomach felt so **abysmal** that I had to drink a bottle of **Pepto-Bismol**.

accede (verb): to express approval for; to give into. "uh SEED"

Think: **agreed**.

Since we all **accede** to the plan to seed the garden, it looks like we're **agreed**.

accolade (noun): an expression of praise. "AK oh lade"

Think: **Escalade**.

I received many **accolades** for my service, but my favorite was the gift of a brand-new Cadillac **Escalade**.

accretion (noun): growth via a gradual buildup.
"uh CREE shun"

Think: **creeps up on**.

Gaining weight **creeps up on** a lot of people since they don't notice the slow **accretion** of fat.

accumulate (verb): to gradually increase.
"Ah KYOOM you late"

Think: **cumulus** clouds.

We better pack up this picnic and leave - those **cumulus** clouds are **accumulating** and I think there's gonna be a thunderstorm soon.

acerbic (adjective): harsh; biting. "uh SIR bick"

Think: **acidic**.

On American Idol, Simon Cowell's criticism was **acerbic** to the point of being **acidic**.

acidulous (adjective): somewhat harsh. "uh SID you luss"

Think: **acid-ish**.

I like Sour Patch Kids because their **acidulous** taste is **acid-ish** without being too painful.

acme (noun): the highest point of something "ACK me"

Think: **acne**.

In high school, I was plagued by **acne**: the **acme** of my nose was often a giant zit.

acquisitive (adjective): eager to acquire and possess; greedy. "uh QUIZ zit tive"

Think: **a squid visited**.

An **acquisitive squid visited** my house and wrapped his arms around all of my valuable Chinese porcelain.

acrimonious (adjective): bitter. "ak rih MOAN ee us"

Think: **a crime on us**.

Committing **a crime on us** makes us **acrimonious**.

acumen (noun): insightfulness. "AK you min"

Think: **accurate men**.

In business, **accurate men** usually have **acumen**.

adamant (adjective): stubborn; unyielding. "AD uh mint"

Think: **Adam...damn it!**

God was **adamant** that **Adam** not return to the Garden of Eden: "I said no, **damn it!**"

adept (adjective): very skilled. "uh DEPPED"

Think: **adapt**.

Mountain lions can **adapt** to almost any climate and environment; they're **adept** at survival.

adequate (adj): appropriate; good enough. "AD uh quit"

Think: **had to quit.**

I **had to quit** at mile 15 of my marathon, but now that I think about it, 15 miles is plenty **adequate** for a solid workout.

adhere (verb): to stick to something. "ad HERE"

Think: **adhesive**.

The **adhesive** on the Band-Aid made it **adhere** to my finger.

admonished (verb): warned to do what's best.
"ad MON isht"

Think: **add Monistat**.

"**Add Monistat** to your body if you're suffering from a vaginal yeast infection," the ad **admonished**.

adorned (adjective): decorated. "uh DORNED"

Think: **add ornaments**.

If you adore Christmas, then you probably enjoy **adorning** your home by **adding ornaments** to your tree.

adroit (adjective): skillful.
"uh DROIT" (rhymes with "Detroit")

Think: **a Droid**.

A Droid is an **adroit** cell phone since it can do so much.

adulation (noun): excessive admiration. "ad joo LAY shun"

Think: **adult adoration**.

The grown **adult's adoration** of role-playing video games could only be called **adulation**.

adulterate (verb): to corrupt; to make impure.
"uh DULT er ate"

Think: **adultery**.

In The Bible, God said, "Thou shalt not commit **adultery**." because an affair will **adulterate** a marriage.

adversary (noun): an enemy or rival. "AD ver sare ee"

Think: **adversity**

Israel faces more **adversity** than most countries; it is nearly completely bordered with **adversaries**.

advocate (noun:) supporter, ally. "AD voh kit"

Think: **I voted**.

I voted in the election, proving I'm an **advocate** of our democracy.

aegis (noun): protection. "EE gis"

Think: **egg us**

Go ahead, try to **egg us** - our house has the **aegis** of the police, since my dad's a cop.

aesthetic (adjective): relating to beauty.
"es THE tick" (rhymes with "pathetic")

Think: **athletic** body.

If you're **athletic**, then you're likely to have a body that is **aesthetic**ally pleasing.

affable (adjective): friendly. "AFF uh bull"

Think: **laughable**.

Since they want tourists to feed them, zoo **giraffes** are so **affable** that it's **laughable**.

affectation (noun): an artificial way of behaving.
"aff eck TAY shun"

Think: **a fake fiction**.

Madonna's phony English accent is an **affectation**; it is **a fake fiction**.

affiliated (adjective): related to, intertwined.
"uh FILL ee ate ed"

Think: **Philly I ate**.

When I went to **Philly I ate** a cheesesteak, because cheesesteaks are **affiliated** with Philadelphia.

affront (noun): an insult or offense. "uh FRONT"

Think: **afro in front**.

I have a huge **afro**, so if I sit **in front** of people at a movie, they often take it as an **affront**.

aggrandized (verb): made greater; enhanced.
"uh GRAND ized"

Think: **a grand-sized**.

I **aggrandized** my social status by throwing a lavish party - it gave me **a grand-sized** reputation.

aghast (adjective): struck by fear or amazement.
"uh GASSED"

Think: **a ghost**.

I was **aghast** when I looked in the mirror and saw **a ghost** standing next to me.

alacrity (noun): cheerful promptness. "uh LACK crih tee"

Think: **electricity**.

Electricity has **alacrity,** since it only takes a millisecond for the light to come on after I flip the switch.

algorithm (noun): a mathematical formula or procedure. "AL guh rhythm"

Think: **Al Gore's rhythm.**

It's an inconvenient truth that, on the dance floor, **Al Gore's rhythm** is as dull and predictable as a computer **algorithm**.

alleviate (verb): to soothe or lessen the severity of. "uh LEAVE ee ate"

Think: **Aleve.**

Allison's headache was so bad that she took four **Aleve** pills to **alleviate** the pain.

allusion (noun): an indirect reference. "al LEW shun"

Think: **A lewd sin.**

"Adjusting the antenna" is one of the funnier allusions to what some might consider **a lewd sin.**

altruistic (adjective): unselfish concern for others. "al true IST ick"

Think: **always true stick**.

My wingman is **altruistic**: he's **always true** to me and will **stick** by my side when I hit on chicks - even if he's not interested in any of them.

amalgamate (verb): unify; join parts into a whole. "uh MAL gum ate"

Think: **gum**.

After breaking the vase, **Malcolm** used **gum** to **amalgamate** the pieces back together.

ambiguity (noun): The state of being unclear or ambiguous. "am big YOU it ee"

Think: **a big "U" for undecided**.

When it came time to indicate her political party on the ballot, Virginia checked neither a big "D" for Democrat, nor a big "R" for Republican, but instead, **a big "U" for undecided** due to her **ambiguity**.

ambivalence (noun): contradictory feelings toward something. "am BIV ull ents"

Think: **valence electron**.

The **valence electron** was **ambivalent** about which electrons he wanted to pair off with. According to his mother, he was **unsure** and afraid of commitment.

ameliorated (verb): made better. "uh MEAL ee or ate id"

Think: **Emilio rated**.

Emilio rated my pasta as a 10 out of 10, which **ameliorated** my fear that I had ruined it.

amenable (adjective): willing; cooperative. "uh MEN uh BULL"

Think: **amen-able**.

After she shouted **"amen!"**, I was able to tell that she was **amenable** to my plan.

amicable (adjective): friendly. "AM ick uh bull"

Think: **hammock-able**.

When **Amy** reminded me that her **hammock** was **able** to hold two people, I knew that she was **amicable**.

amortize (verb): to gradually pay off or reduce.
"am MORT eyes"

Think: **a mortgage.**

Unless you have a ton of money, when you buy a house, you probably **amortize** the loan with **a mortgage**.

ample (adjective): enough or more than enough.
"AM pull"

Think: **Apple.**

With about $200 billion in cash reserves (in 2015), **Apple** has **ample** resources.

anachronism (noun): something belonging to a different time period. "an NACK ron is im"

Think: **inaccurate chronology.**

The movie has something **inaccurate** about its **chronology**: a caveman wearing a watch - a huge **anachronism**.

analogue (noun): something similar. "an al LOG"

Think: **Analog vs. Digital.**

My audiophile cousin swears that **analog** is way better than **digital**, but to me they sound pretty **similar**.

anathema (noun): something hated; a curse.
"uh NATH em uh"

Think: **a nasty enema**.

If a patient is constipated, then **a nasty enema** may follow, which can be **anathema** for the nurse.

anile (adjective): senile. "ANN ile" (rhymes with "dial")

Think: **senile**.

I knew my Aunt Ann was **anile** to the point of being **senile** when she asked to go swimming in the Nile.

animosity (noun): hatred; hostility. "an ih MOSS ih tee"

Think: **enemy city**.

During the war, I accidentally parachuted into the **enemy city** and was met with **animosity**.

annotation (noun): a comment or note on a literary work.
"ann oh TAY shun"

Think: **a notation**.

There are lots of **annotations** in my copy of *Hamlet*; I made **a notation** every time I needed to define an unfamiliar term.

annul (verb): to cancel. "ann ULL"

Think: **null set**.

In mathematics, the **null set** means "a set that contains nothing." If you **annul (cancel)** your marriage, you end it.

anodyne (noun): a pain-reliever. "ann oh DINE"

Think: **am not dying**.

I have the flu, but my doctor-prescribed **anodyne** finally has made me feel like I **am not dying**.

anomaly (noun): something unusual. "uh NOM uh lee"

Think: **abnormally knobby knee**.

I have an **abnormally knobby knee**; my doctor tells me it's an **anomaly**.

antedate (verb): to come before. "AN tuh date"

Think: **auntie ante- (before) date**.

Chances are that your **auntie** has a birth **date** that **antedates** yours.

antediluvian (adjective): ancient; primitive.
"ann tee die LOUVE ee in"

Think: **anti-dildo-lovin'**.

Only someone with **antediluvian** views on sex would be **anti-dildo-lovin'**.

antipode (noun): the exact opposite. "ANN tih pode"

Think: **anti-pole**.

The North **Pole** is the **antipode** to the South **Pole** - you might say they're "**anti-poles**."

antithesis (noun): opposite. "ann TITH uh sis"

Think: **anti-thesis**.

You got a "D" on your essay because your examples argued for the **antithesis** of your introduction's **thesis**.

apace (adverb): quickly. "uh PACE"

Think: **keep pace**.

The Indy 500 racer's pit crew changed his tires **apace** so he could **keep pace** with the leaders.

apartheid (noun): the policy of separating groups based on race. "uh PAR thighed"

Think: **apart to hide.**

In South Africa, **apartheid** kept blacks **apart to hide** them from racist whites.

aplomb (noun): confidence. "uh PLOM"

Think: the **bomb.**

If you have **aplomb**, you think you're the **bomb.**

apocryphal (adjective): of doubtful truthfulness. "uh POCK rih full"

Think: **apocalypse** predictions.

The prediction that the **apocalypse** would happen in 2012 turned out to be **apocryphal.**

apoplectic (adjective): enraged. "ah puh PLEK tick"

Think: **Apu epileptic.**

In the Simpsons, when Nelson robbed his Kwik-E-Mart, **Apu** shook with **apoplectic** rage as if he was having an **epileptic** seizure.

apostle (noun): a supporter. "uh PAH sill"

Think: **A posse.**

The famous rapper was known to roll deep with his many **apostles** – his **posse**, that is.

apothegm (noun): a short, wise remark. "APP uh THEM"

Think: **pocket the gem.**

"**Pocket the gem!**" is a good **apothegm** to remember if you're training to be a jewelry store robber.

apotheosis (noun): a perfect example. "uh POTH ee oh sis"

Think: **a potent thesis.**

My professor said he gave me only A in the class because my paper was the **apotheosis** of a persuasive essay: it had **a potent thesis**.

appease (verb): to soothe, satisfy or pacify. "uh PEAS"

Think: **please** with **peas.**

I **appease** and **please** my baby daughter by hiding her **peas** inside of her mashed potatoes.

apportion (verb): to divide and distribute. "uh POOR shun"

Think: **a portion.**

If you want **a portion** of lunch, go ask the lunch lady - she **apportions** it to everyone.

apposite (adjective): appropriate. "APP uh sit"

Think: **a positive site.**

Wikipedia is **a positive site** because it's **apposite** for all kinds of research.

approbation (noun): approval; praise. "app pro BAY shun"

Think: **approve probation.**

Maybe the best **approbation** I ever received was when the judge finally **approved** me for **probation.**

apropos (adjective): relevant. "app pro POH"

Think: **appropriate.**

It's **apropos** and **appropriate** that we're talking about **posing** because I was just discovered and contracted to be a model!

arbitrary (adjective): done without reason; random. "ARE bit TRARE ee"

Think: **varies a bit.**

When I order a pizza, the amount of toppings I get often seems pretty **arbitrary** – it always **varies a bit**.

arcane (adjective): mysterious; known only to a few. "are CANE"

Think: **Ark of the Covenant.**

Indiana Jones understood the **arcane Ark of the Covenant**; the Nazis did not, which is why they perished.

arch (adjective): sassy. "arch"

Think: **arched eyebrow.**

Her playful, **arch** comment made me **arch** my eyebrow.

archaic (adjective): no longer current; outdated. "are KAY ick"

Think: **arch age.**

I knew you time-traveled here from the Roman Empire because your **archaic** expressions sound like you're from the **arch age**.

arduous (adjective): strenuous; difficult. "ARE joo us"

Think: **hard for us**.

Clearing out that hoarder's house is **arduous**; it's **hard for us** because he kept every piece of junk mail he ever received.

arid (adjective): very dry. "AIR rid"

Think: **Arrid** Extra Dry.

"Get a little closer; don't be shy! Get a little closer, with **Arrid** Extra Dry deodorant (which keeps your armpits **arid**)!"

arrogate (verb): to unrightfully take or claim. "ARE uh gate"

Think: **a rogue ate**.

My liege – **a rogue ate** my rations – may I have more since he **arrogated** what was rightfully mine?

articulate (adjective): using clear, expressive language. "are TICK you lit"

Think: **article**.

Oscar Wilde was so **articulate** that his conversational speech could be used as a newspaper **article** without any editing.

artifice (noun): deception; trickery. "ART ih fiss"

Think: **artificial**.

In *The Hunger Games*, Effie Trinket tries to win people over with **artifice**, but it doesn't work because her sweetness is so **artificial**.

artless (adjective): simple; without cunning. "ART less"

Think: **art-less** flirting.

Flirting is an **art** I use **less** than most people; it's definitely pretty **artless** when I just go up to a girl and tell her I like her.

ascendancy (noun): governing or controlling influence. "Uh SEND and see".

Think: **ascend and see.**

In battles, armies strive to take hills: **ascending** to higher ground makes it easier to see one's enemy and leads to tactical **ascendancy**.

ascetic (adjective): practicing self-denial. "uh SET ick"

Think: **asset? ick!**

The **ascetic** Buddhist monk, when offered the chance to take money or another **asset**, said **"ick!"**

ashen (adjective): very pale. "ASH in"

Think: **ash.**

When he saw the ghost, his complexion became so **ashen** that his face was the color of **ash**.

askew (adjective): slanted to one side. "uh SKEW"

Think: **skew.**

Your picture is **askew** because the earthquake **skewed** it from hanging evenly.

asperity (noun): bad temper. "ass PEAR it ee"

Think: **a spear in me**.

I have **asperity** because I have **a spear in me** – can you blame me?

aspersion (noun): a false claim intended to harm. "ass SPUR shun"

Think: **asp poison**.

Her **aspersions** about what I did last night felt like **asp poison**.

aspiration (noun): a hope or ambition. "asp ear A shun"

Think: **as a pirate.**

As a pirate, I'll be able to fulfill my **aspiration** of sailing the high seas and robbing the rich.

assail (verb): to attack violently. "ass SALE"

Think: **ass sail**.

Come at me, bro: if I **assail** you, I'll make your **ass sail** out the window.

assiduous (adjective): hardworking; dedicated. "ass SID you us"

Think: **assist us**.

Assiduous Sid worked his **ass** off to **assist us**.

assuage: (verb): to make less severe. "uh SWAJ"

Think: **massage**.

astray: (adj): away from the correct path; into error. "ass TRAY"

Think: **a stray dog.**

A stray dog has gone **astray** from its family.

astute (adjective): clever. "ass TOOT"

Think: **SAT student**.

I had an **SAT student** named Stu who was so **astute** that he got a 1600 on the **SAT**.

attenuate (verb): to reduce. "at TEN you ate"

Think: **ten to eight**.

If you go from **ten** drinks a week to **eight** drinks a week, then you've **attenuated** your number of beverages.

audacious (adjective): fearlessly bold; arrogantly bold. "awe DAY shus"

Think: **awed us**.

Walking up to Obama and swiping his pen as he was about to sign the bill was so **audacious** that it **awed us**.

augment (verb): to increase the size of or to improve. "awwg MEANT"

Think: **Aug. meant**.

The arrival of **Aug. meant** that the colonists could **augment** their food storage by harvesting maize.

august (adjective): majestic. "awe GUST"

Think: **Augustus** Caesar.

Augustus Caesar, the first Roman emperor, was so **august** that they named a month after him.

auspicious (adjective): favorable. "awe SPISH us"

Think: **suspicious** I'm **awesome**.

Dude, the chances she'll go out with me are **auspicious** or "**awe**-spicious" because I'm suspicious that I'm **awesome**.

austere (adjective): plain; strict; serious; cold. "awe STEER"

Think: **Austria stern**.

Life among the Alps in **Austria** is **stern** and **austere** - it's hard to party when there's a wind chill of -20.

authoritative (adjective): having impressive knowledge about a subject; confident. "Auth OR it tay tive".

Think: **author**.

The reason we can speak **authoritatively** about GRE Vocab Capacity is that we wrote it: we're the **authors**.

automaton (noun): one who acts in a robotic way. "awe tah mah tahn" (rhymes with "on")

Think: **automation**.

Working on assembly line where **automation** has replaced creativity can make you feel like an **automaton**.

autonomous (adjective): operating independently. "awe tahn nom us"

Think: **Auto no mo' us**.

With the advent of self-driving **autos** like the Google car, the cars won't be needing **us no mo'**.

avaricious (adjective): greedy. "ave uh RISH us"

Think: **have our riches**.

My boy band and I don't trust you as an agent - you're **avaricious** and just want to **have our riches**.

aver (verb): to state confidently; to declare. "uh VAIR"

Think: **verify**.

After I **verify** that the blood sample from the crime scene matches your DNA, I'll **aver** that you are the killer.

aversion (noun): A tendency to avoid or dislike. "uh VER shun"

Think: **cover versions**.

I have an **aversion** to **cover version**s of songs – I almost always prefer the original tune.

avuncular (adjective): like an uncle. "uh VUNK you lure"

Think: **uncle**.

The **avuncular** professor was like an **uncle** to him, dispensing well-intentioned advice.

badger (verb): to annoy or pester. "BAD jur"

Think: **bad jerk**.

Good jerks can get laughs, but a **bad jerk** will just **badger** you with his attempts at humor.

baleful (adjective): threatening harm. "BALE full"

Think: **Christian Bale**.

I'm not a big Christian **Bale** fan – he always has that **baleful** look on his face, like he wants to start a **fight** with you.

banal (adjective): unoriginal. "buh NALL"

Think: **ban all**.

The **banal** librarian thought there were enough books already and wanted to **ban all** the new ones.

base (adjective): not honest or good; having low quality or value. (rhymes with "face")

Think: **basement**.

I live in my mom's **basement**, but I don't list that on my OkCupid profile: there's an unfortunate stereotype that people who live in **basements** tend to be **base**.

battery (noun): a large group of similar things. "BAT er ee"

Think: **batter - y**.

I thought that my first mix of cupcake **batter** tasted a little too **batter-y**, so I put it through a **battery** of taste tests before baking my final batch.

bauble (noun): a small, inexpensive piece of jewelry or toy. "BAW bull"

Think: **bobblehead**.

The **bauble** that my favorite baseball player gave me was a **bobblehead** of himself.

baying (verb): shouting. "BAY ing"

Think: **Michael Bay movie.**

Even though I was in the other room, I could tell my roommates were watching a **Michael Bay movie**, like Transformers, because of all the **baying** from the T.V.

beatific (adjective): extremely happy. "bee TIH fick"

Think: **beautiful! terrific!**

If you feel **beatific**, you probably walk around exclaiming, "**beautiful! terrific!**" all day.

beatify (verb): to bless; to make happy. "BEE tih fie"

Think: **beautiful** home = happiness.

The makeover will **beautify** your home and **beatify** your family.

becalm (verb): to make motionless; to soothe. "buh KAHM"

Think: **be calm!**

When my 3-year-old is running around causing havoc, I usually whisper "**be calm!**" to **becalm** him.

bedlam (noun): a state of uproar and confusion. "BED lum"

Think: **bed lamb**.

It was complete **bedlam** when I entered my hotel room and saw that the **bed** had a **lamb** sleeping in it.

beguile (verb): to trick. "buh GILE" (rhymes with "dial")

Think: **be gullible**.

Be gullible, and you'll be easy to **beguile**.

behemoth (noun): something huge. "buh HE mith"

Think: **beast mammoth**.

One really large **beast** was the woolly **mammoth**, a **behemoth** that lived during the Ice Age.

beleaguered (adjective): weary, tired, bothered. "bee LEE gerd"

Think: **B - Leaguer**.

"I'm **sick and tired** of being a **B-leaguer** instead of an A-Leaguer," said the B-movie actor.

belied (verb): contradicted. "buh LIED"

Think: **lied.**

The used car salesman's smooth manner was **belied** by his sweaty handshake and made me think, "He **lied**!"

belittle (verb): to put down; to disparage. "bee LITTLE"

Think: **be little.**

When you say "Good boy!" and pat me on head, you **belittle** me and make me feel as if I **be little.**

bellicose (adjective): warlike; inclined to fight. "BELL ih kose"

Think: **belly bellow.**

"ARRGHH!" When I heard the beast's **belly bellow**, I knew it was **bellicose.**

bemoan (verb): to mourn over; to express grief for. "bee MOAN"

Think: **moan.**

I **be moanin'** about the new laws restricting what we can smoke - my friends **bemoan** the legislation, too.

beneficence (noun): the quality of being kind or charitable. "buh NIF uh sense"

Think: **benefit sent**.

Through the **beneficence** of musicians like Paul McCartney and Sting, the **benefit** concert **sent** millions of dollars to starving children.

benign (adjective): harmless. "Bee NINE"

Think: **be nice.**

It would **be nice** if the lump on my arm is **benign** instead of cancerous.

bereft (adjective): deprived or robbed of something. "bee REFT"

Think: **he left**.

After **he left** her at the altar and crushed her dreams, she felt completely **bereft**.

beseech (verb): to beg or ask. "bee SEACH"

Think: **screech**.

Forget fancy language – the best way to **beseech** someone is to **screech** at him.

bifurcated (verb): split in two. "BY fur kated"

Think: **by forking**.

By forking, the road **bifurcated** into the popular road and the road less traveled by.

bilious (adjective): bad-tempered. "BILL ee iss"

Think: **bully us**.

We goth kids are only **bilious** because the jocks like to **bully us**.

blase (adjective): apathetic; unconcerned. "blah SAY"

Think: **blah say**.

I'm a rock star, so I'm **blase** and **"blah blah blah"** is all I **say** even when blazingly hot girls try to talk to me.

blithe (adjective): happy, casual, unconcerned. "blythe"

Think: **glide**.

He just **glides** through life – he's so **blithe**.

bloviated (verb): was wordy/windy when speaking. "BLOW vee ate ed"

Think: **blow** hot air.

In Harry Potter, Gilderoy Lockhart **bloviated**; he would **blow** a lot of hot air without much meaning.

bludgeon (verb): to hit forcefully. "BLUJ in"

Think: **Bludgers**.

In Quidditch, the **Bludgers** are 10-inch, black, iron balls that fly around and sometimes **bludgeon** players.

bonhomie (noun): a pleasant and friendly mood. "bahn nom EE"

Think: **abundance** of **homies**.

When I have an **abundance** of **homies**, I have **bonhomie**.

boon (noun): a benefit. "boon"

Think: **booing**.

One **boon** of **booing** is that it unites an audience in mutual unappreciation.

boor (noun): a crude person with rude, clumsy manners. "boar"

Think: **boar** manners.

The **boor** had table manners like a wild **boar** and ate directly off the plate with his mouth.

bootless (adjective): useless. "BOOT less"

Think: **booty-less**.

A **booty-less** pirate is probably a **bootless** pirate.

bowdlerize (verb): to cut out all the offensive parts of a book. "BOWED lure eyes"

Think: **boulder-ize**.

Originally, they would **bowdlerize** Huckleberry Finn so much that they might as well have let **boulders** roll over the book and tear out half the pages.

bravado (noun): a false show of bravery; swagger. "bruh VAH doe"

Think: **brave avocado**.

Though its trash-talking seemed **brave**, the **avocado** and its **bravado** didn't scare me, since I knew it was just a piece of fruit.

brazen (adjective): shamelessly bold. "BRAY zen"

Think: **blazin'**.

Blazin' up a joint during class is certainly **brazen**, but it'll get you expelled 100 out of 100 times.

brevity (noun): shortness of duration. "BREV it ee"

Think: **abbreviate**.

I know your speech is brief but **abbreviate** it even more - this professor actually awards points for **brevity**.

bromide (noun): a cliché or tired saying. "BRO myed"

Think: **bro lied**.

My **bro** on the lacrosse team told me to "give 110 percent," but the next day my math teacher told me that was impossible. **Bro lied** in his **bromide**.

brusque (adjective): abrupt; curt; harsh. "brusk"

Think: **brushed** off.

I tried to make friends with the club's bouncer, but he was **brusque** and **brushed** me off.

bucolic (adjective): rustic; rural. "byoo CAA lick"

Think: **blue collar**.

I'm just a **bucolic** broccoli farmer - a **blue collar** worker - I don't understand what those suits are talking about!

bugbear (noun): something to fear. "BUG bear"

Think: **bug** a **bear**.

If you **bug** a **bear**, you'll soon have a very serious **bugbear**.

bulwark (adjective): a strong support or protection. "BOOL work"

Think: **bull work**.

In a bullfighting arena, the barrier to protect the spectators from the **bull** better **work**; it has to be a **bulwark**.

bumptious (adjective): assertive in a loud, arrogant way. "BUMP shus"

Think: **bump us**.

You're the type of guy who would push past us in a crowd and **bump us** and not say you're sorry – you're **bumptious**.

bungle (verb): to screw up. "BUNG gull"

Think: **bunghole.**

I **bungled** the job so many times that they started calling me a "**bunghole**".

buoyant (adjective): happy; confident. "BOY ent"

Think: **boo-yah!**

If you hear someone yell "**boo-yah!**" then you can bet she's feeling **buoyant**.

burdensome (adjective): oppressive; causing difficulty or worry. "BIRD den sum"

Think: **bird dim sum.**

The decor of this Chinese restaurant is nice, except for the giant vulture circling our table. The **burdensome** feeling that **bird** gives me makes it hard for me to enjoy my **dim sum**.

burgeoning (adjective): growing. "BURJ un ing"

Think: **burgers.**

If you eat too many **burgers**, your waistline will be **burgeoning**.

buttress (noun): a support. "BUT ress"

Think: **butt rest**.

The stone column is both a **buttress** and a **butt rest** for tired people to lean against.

bygone (adjective): past. "BY gone"

Think: **bye gone**.

The **bygone** days of my childhood are days I've said **bye** to cause they're **gone**.

byzantine (adjective): devious; complicated. "BIZ in teen"

Think: **busy ant**.

Only the **busy ant** will be able to make its way through the **byzantine** maze you've created.

cache (noun): a secure storage place or something in that place. "kah SHAY"

Think: **cash** hiding place.

The drug dealer kept his **cash** in a **cache** under the bed - he didn't trust banks.

cacophony (noun): a harsh, unharmonious sound. "kuh KAW fun ee"

Think: **cough symphony**.

The sounds from the tuberculosis ward were a **cacophony** - an unpleasant **cough symphony**.

cadge (verb): to beg or get via begging. "cadj"

Think: locked in a **cage**.

If you're locked in a **cage**, you'll **cadge** for food and water.

cajole (verb): to coax. "ka JOLE"

Think: **cage hole**.

At the vet, I have to **cajole** my cat out of the **cage hole** so he can get examined.

calamitous (adjective): related to a terrible event. "ka LAM it us"

Think: **calamari vomit**.

It's **calamitous** when you eat undercooked **calamari**, become **vomitous**, and puke on your date.

callous (adjective): unsympathetic; hard-hearted. "KAL us"

Think: **callus**.

The **callous** dictator thought nothing of executing his rivals; he must have had a **callus** on his soul.

callow (adjective): inexperienced; immature. "KAL owe"

Think: **shallow**.

Popping her gum while reading Cosmo, the **callow** teenager was **shallow** only because she hadn't seen much of the world yet.

calumnious (adjective): slanderous, defamatory, an untrue statement intended to injure one's reputation. "kuh-LUM-nee-us"

Think: gossip **column**.

The author of the famous gossip **column** was less concerned with provoking lawsuits through his **calumnious** statements than he was with attracting hordes of readers through salacious headlines.

camaraderie (noun): togetherness. "com uh ROD er ee"

Think: **comrades**.

The Russian camera factory workers shared a sense of **camaraderie**, calling each other **comrades**.

canard (noun): a false report or rumor. "cuh NARD"

Think: **Qatar**.

There's a widespread **canard** that **Qatar** bribed FIFA to host the World Cup.

canny (adjective): clever. "CAN knee"

Think: **can knee**.

I'm **canny** because I **can** use my **knee** to drive my car when I need both hands for something else.

canonize (verb): to make a saint (literal) or to put someone beyond reproach (figurative). "CAN nun eyes"

Think: **can on ice**.

In order to properly **canonize** St. Patrick, one must keep a beer **can on ice** at all times.

capacious (adjective): spacious. "ka PAY shus"

Think: Batman's **cape** is **spacious**.

Batman is a big guy, so his **cape** is **spacious** and **capacious**.

capitulate (verb): to surrender. "ka PIT chew late"

Think: **capsized? it's too late**.

Once your boat has **capsized**, **it's too late** to think about winning the race: **capitulate** and just try not to drown.

capricious (adjective): impulsive; done without forethought. "ka PRISH us"

Think: **capri pants**.

Jenny made the **capricious** decision to buy five pairs of **capri pants**, which she later regretted when they went out of style.

captious (adjective): overly critical. "CAP shus"

Think: red **CAPS**.

Our English teacher is **captious**: our papers come back with lots of red writing that's in all **CAPS**.

cardinal (adjective): of main importance. "KAR din ull"

Think: **cardinal** bird.

You'd think the bright red male **cardinal** (noun) was the most **cardinal** (adjective) bird because of its vivid color.

caricatured (verb): distorted, often comically.
"Care ick cah chured"

Think: **cartoon character.**

Check out any political **cartoon character** and you'll see someone **caricatured**: any cartoon of Trump will have enormous hair.

castigate (verb): to criticize severely. "KAS tig ate"

Think: **castrate**.

The worst way for a Mafia boss to **castigate** someone is to **castrate** him.

caterwaul (verb): to cry or to complain loudly.
"CAT tur wall"

Think: **cat in wall**.

If there's a **cat in** your **wall** it will probably **caterwaul** since it wants to get out.

causal (adjective): relating to the cause of something or causing something. "KAW zul"

Think: **cause.**

There is a **causal** link between laziness and poor grades; being lazy **causes** less studying and therefore lower marks. (Don't confuse causal with casual).

celerity (noun): quickness. "suh lear it ee"

Think: **accelerate.**

After Cee Lo switched to an all-celery diet, he lost 30 pounds and his ability to **accelerate** increased, as did his **celerity**.

censure (verb): to criticize harshly. "SEN sure"

Think: **censor.**

If you really wanted to **censure** your rival's editorial you could just **censor** it completely.

cerebral (adjective): intellectual. "suh REE brul"

Think: **cerebrum.**

Einstein was so **cerebral** that they studied the **cerebrum** of his brain after he died.

chagrin (noun): distress caused by disappointment. "shuh GRIN"

Think: **chuggin' tragic.**

You won't believe this, but to my **chagrin**, Chad is **chuggin'** a bottle of mouthwash right now – this is a **tragic** date.

champion (verb): to fight for. "CHAM pee in"

Think: **champion** (noun).

If you **champion** (verb) that turtle in the turtle race and cheer for her really loudly, it's more likely she'll become the **champion** (noun).

chary (adjective): very cautious. "cherry"

Think: **chair-wary.**

My brothers were always pulling my **chair** away as I was about to sit down, so now I'm **chary**, or **chair-wary.**

chicanery (noun): trickery. "shi CAN er ee"

Think: **chick-gain-ery**

Your frat brother's feigned interest in that cute girl's paintings was clearly **chicanery**; his motive was "**chick-gain-ery**".

choleric (adjective): irritable. "CALL er ick"

Think: **cholera.**

I'd be **choleric** too if someone's fecal matter made me get **cholera.**

chronological (adjective): ordered by time. "kron oh LAH ji kull"

Think: **chron = time.**

The Houston **Chronicle** is a newspaper that, like any good journal, reports events in **chronological** order. All its reporters wear **chronometers** (watches) to keep track of their deadlines.

churlish (adjective): rude; difficult. "CHURL ish"

Think: **church lush.**

The **church lush** usually showed up to mass stumbling drunk, inviting us to call him **churlish.**

cinematic (adjective): suggestive of a movie. "Sin im AT tick"

Think: **cinema.**

The video you shot on your iPhone is **cinematic** enough to be shown in a **cinema.**

circuitous (adjective): roundabout; not direct.
"sir KYOO it us"

Think: **circuit-ish**.

The crooked cabdriver took a **circuitous** route; his path was **circuit-ish** to increase the fare.

circumscribed (adjective): restricted. "SIR kum skribed"

Think: **circumference scribe**.

The evil **scribe** drew a magical **circumference** around our campsite, which **circumscribed** our movement to that circle.

circumspect (adjective): cautious. "sir kum SPECT"

Think: **circle inspect**.

When you rent a car, walk in a **circle** to **inspect** it for dents; if you're not **circumspect** now, they may charge you later.

circumvents (verb): avoids; gets around something.
"sir kum VENTS"

Think: **circumference vents**.

She **circumvents** the guards by crawling around the enemy base's **circumference** through the **vents**.

clairvoyant (adjective): able to see the future.
"clare VOY int"

Think: **clear voyage**.

My trusted psychic, Miss Cleo, assured me that rowing a boat from California to Hawaii would work out just fine. "I see a **clear voyage** in your future," said the **clairvoyant** woman.

clandestine (adjective): secret. "klan DEST in"

Think: **clan** of **destiny**.

Because we're the **clan** of **destiny**, we have to keep our meetings **clandestine** – otherwise, the empire will kill us all.

clangorous (adjective): loud; noisy. "KLAYNG er us"

Think: **clang**.

The disinterested 3rd graders in the school band **clanged** on their instruments as hard as they could, producing a **clangorous** racket.

clemency (noun): mercy. "KLEM in see"

Think: **Clemens mercy**.

The pitcher Roger **Clemens** was shown **mercy** by the jury and found not guilty - an act of **clemency**, since he was accused of taking steroids.

climatic (adjective): pertaining to climate and weather.

Think: **dramatic**.

Due to global warming, **climatic** events such as hurricanes and floods have been much more **dramatic** in recent years. (Don't confuse with "climactic", which refers to the climax of a work of art.)

climax (noun): the most intense, exciting, or important part of something. "CLY max"

Think: **climb ax**.

The **climax** of our ascent of Mt. Everest was definitely reaching the summit; our **climb ax** enabled us to scramble up the final few feet.

cloying (adjective): gross because it's too much.
"KLOY ing"

Think: **annoying**.

Always talking baby-talk to each other, the couple was so **annoying** that they were **cloying**.

coalesce (verb): to unite into a whole. "koh uh LESS"

Think: **coal essence**.

Coal, in **essence**, is just carbon – if you squeeze it hard enough it will **coalesce** into a diamond.

cocksure (adjective): overconfident.
"KOCK (rhymes with "dock") sure"

Think: **cocky** and **sure**.

The baseball rookie was so **cocky** and **sure** that he'd hit a home run during his first at-bat that he was **cocksure**.

coddle (adjective): to treat with excessive care. "KOD ul"

Think: **cuddle**.

The mother dog would **coddle** and **cuddle** her puppy so much that I thought it would never learn to fend for itself.

coerced (verb): forced. "co URSED"

Think: **cooperate** by **force**.

I didn't want to leave the bar, but the bouncer **coerced** me to **cooperate** by using **force**.

coeval (adjective): existing at the same time, contemporary. "Coh EE vill"

Think: **co-evil.**

Hitler, Mussolini, and Franco, three of history's most **evil** rulers, were **coeval** because they all lived during the same era.

cognizant (adjective): aware; informed. "KOG nih zent"

Think: **recognize.**

If you're **cognizant** of our theory, you must **recognize** where our solution came from.

coherence (noun): the quality of being understandable. "Co HERE ents"

Think: **can hear it.**

Public Speaking 101 taught me that the first rule of **coherence** when giving a speech is speaking loudly - make sure your audience **can hear it.**

70

cohesive (adjective): holding together well.
"co HEESE ive"

Think: **adhesive**.

A **cohesive** argument holds together even when attacked –
as if it's strengthened by an **adhesive**.

cohort (noun): a friend or companion.
"KOH hort (rhymes with "short")"

Think: **co-heart**.

My **cohort** and I are so close that it feels more like we're
co-hearts.

coin (verb): to invent a new word or phrase. "KOIN"

Think: **coin** (noun).

Just as the U.S. mint molds metal into a new **coin** (noun),
so we can **coin** (verb) new expressions.

collusion (noun): the process of working together to
deceive, often illegally by businesses. "cuh LUGE un"

Think: **co-illusion.**

When the world's two main exporters of oil decided to
create the **co-illusion** of scarcity when there was none, the
media accused them of price gouging and **collusion**.

commensurate (adjective): equal or proportionate.
"kuh MEN sur it"

Think: **co-measure it**.

Our estimates of the carbon content of this dinosaur bone will be **commensurate** if we **co-measure it**.

commiserate (verb): to sympathize with. "co MISS ur ate"

Think: **misery** loves **company**.

Come **commiserate** with us - **misery** loves **company**.

companionable (adjective): sociable; friendly.
"kum PAN yin uh bull"

Think: **companion-able**.

Most dogs are **companionable** and love people; that's why they're so **able** to be **companions**.

complicit (adjective): involved in a crime. "kum PLISS it"

Think: **accomplice**.

Though I robbed the bank and my **accomplice** just drove me there, he was considered **complicit** by the law.

composure (noun): calmness. "kum POSE ure"

Think: **composer's calm pose**.

Even though he was performing his music for kings and queens, the **composer's calm pose** showed his **composure**.

compunction (noun): regret, remorse. "com PUNK shun"

Think: **punctured** balloon.

I felt **compunction** after accidentally **puncturing** the child's birthday balloon and making him cry.

concession (noun): admitting partial or total defeat. "kuhn SESH in"

Think: **confession**.

After it became apparent that my opponent would win the election, my **concession** speech was basically just a **confession** that I lost.

concoct (verb): to make; to invent to deceive. "kuhn COCKED"

Think: **con cocked**

I've **concocted** a safer plan – we'll **con** the bank teller by showing her a **cocked** (but unloaded) pistol.

concomitant (adjective): accompanying, especially in a less important way. "con COM it ent"

Think: **can come with it**.

Drinking too much carries the **concomitant** risk of depression that **can come with it**.

concord (noun): harmony. "CON kord"

Think: **concurred**.

We all **concurred** that we should go into the grape jelly business, so it's no surprise that our company is enjoying a feeling of **concord**.

concupiscence (noun): strong desire, esp. sexual desire. "con KYOOP uh sense"

Think: **Cupid's essence**.

If you have **concupiscence**, you have **Cupid's essence** running through your veins.

condign (adjective): deserved; appropriate. "con DINE"

Think: **can dig**.

I **can dig** the murderer's conviction because it was **condign**.

condones (verb): allows something that is bad. "con DONES"

Think: **con done**.

The **con done** it because the lazy warden **condones** misbehavin'.

conferred (verb): given to. "kuhn FURD"

Think: **fur coat**.

My great-grandmother's **fur coat** was **conferred** to me in her will.

confiscate (verb): to take something away. "KAHN fiss kate"

Think: **can frisk**.

If I **can frisk** you and feel that you're carrying a weapon, then I'll **confiscate** it.

conflagration (noun): a fire. "con FLUH gray shun"

Think: burning **flag nation**.

There is a debate about the **flag** in our **nation** - is it legal to use the Stars and Stripes for a **conflagration**?

conflate (verb): to confuse. "con FLATE"

Think: **con inflated**.

The **con** artist **inflated** the value of the racehorse by grooming it, making me **conflate** sleek appearance with speed.

confound (verb): to confuse (a person) or mix up (a thing), or as an exclamation ("confounded" only). "kun FOUND"

Think: **can't find.**

I **can't find** my keys anywhere and I'm **confounded** as to where they may be. Where the heck are my **confounded** keys?

conglomerate (verb): to gather into a whole. "kuhn GLAH merr it"

Think: **can gobble it.**

My cookie got smashed into a thousand pieces – I'll have to **conglomerate** them so I **can gobble it.**

conniving (verb): secretly plotting to do bad things. "cun NIVE ing"

Think: mean girls' **knives**.

Mean girls act nice, but don't be **conned**: they're **conniving** to stick **knives** in your back.

connoisseur (noun): an expert; one who knows the subtleties of a subject. "con iss URE"

Think: **can know sir**.

When it comes to breakdancing, call me "**can know sir**" because I'm a **connoisseur** of the art.

conscientious (adjective): driven by the urge to do what's right; careful. "con she ENT shus"

Think: **consciences**.

Conscientious people usually are driven to do good deeds by their **consciences**.

conspicuous (adjective): noticeable. "kun SPICK you us"

Think: **can pick on us**.

Since you're new at this school, here's a tip: don't wear anything **conspicuous**. If the jocks see us wearing anything that stands out, they **can pick on us** more easily.

consternation (noun): confusion; agitation; dismay. "con ster NAY shun"

Think: **concerned nation**.

On 9/11/01, a **concerned nation** stood in **consternation** watching the aftermath of terrorism.

contumacious (adjective): stubbornly disobedient; rebellious. "con too MAY shus"

Think: **contrary tummy**.

I have a **contrary tummy** – it's **contumacious** and gives me indigestion if I try to eat spicy food.

conundrum (noun): a difficult problem. "con NUN drum"

Think: **nun drum**.

Building a **nun drum** is a **conundrum** because nuns don't like loud noises.

conversant (adjective): familiar with. "con VERSE int"

Think: **converse it**.

If you're **conversant** with something, you can **converse** about it intelligently.

copious (adjective): plentiful. "KOPE ee us"

Think: **copy us**.

If the zombie apocalypse happens and we survive, let's hope cloning can **copy us** and make humans more **copious**.

cordial (adjective): affectionate. "KORD jull"

Think: **cordial** (noun).

The alcohol in the **cordial** (noun) made me act more **cordial** (adjective).

cordon (verb): to enclose, either to restrict or to protect. "KORD un"

Think: **cord on**.

Cordon off that area by tying a **cord on** and around all the trees so people know it's off limits.

corroborate (verb): to support with evidence. "kuh ROB er ate"

Think: **co-robber**.

When robbing a bank, use a **co-robber** who will **corroborate** your story.

cosmopolitan (adjective): sophisticated.
"kos muh POL it in"

Think: **Cosmo**.

After reading the dating advice in **Cosmo**, the 14-year-old thought she was quite **cosmopolitan**.

covert (adjective): not openly shown. "co VIRT"

Think: **covered**.

The CIA agent was on a **covert** mission, so he **covered** his true identity.

cowed (adjective): intimidated. "COWD"

Think: **coward**.

The bully was at heart a **coward**: as soon as I stood up to him he was **cowed** into silence.

craven (adjective): cowardly. "KRAY vin"

Think: **Wes Craven**.

My **craven** roommate refused to go to the **Wes Craven** movie – it was way too scary for her.

credence (adjective): belief. "KREED ints"

Think: **Creed is.**

If you tell me that **Creed is** your favorite band, then I won't give any **credence** to your musical judgements.

credulous (adjective): too ready to believe things. "KREDGE uh liss"

Think: **cradle us**.

When we are young children and our parents **cradle us**, we tend to be quite **credulous** – we believe anything they tell us (just ask Santa).

crepuscular (adjective): related to twilight. "cru PUS q lur"

Think: **creepy muscular**.

In the movie <u>Twilight</u>, **creepy**, **muscular** vampires prowl during the **crepuscular** hours of the evening.

crestfallen (adjective): dejected; depressed.
"CREST fall en"

Think: **Crest fallen**.

When I saw that my **Crest** toothpaste had **fallen** off my brush into the sink, I was **crestfallen** since that was a waste of perfectly good toothpaste.

cryptic (adjective): having an unclear or hidden meaning.
"KRYP tick"

Think: **crypt**.

Scrawled in blood on the wall of the mummy's **crypt**, the **cryptic** hieroglyphics both confused and frightened us.

cull (verb): to select; to get rid of what's unneeded.
"KUHL"

Think: **kill**.

We're in a famine, so we need to **cull** the herd and **kill** the sick cattle.

culminate (verb): to reach a point of highest development. "CULL min ate"

Think: **coal mine diamond.**

I remember the old days, when you were just a lump of **coal in the mine** with everybody else. Now, thousands of years of pressure from the Earth's crust have **culminated** in you becoming a diamond!

culpable (adjective): deserving blame. "KULP uh bull"

Think: **culprit.**

Unsurprisingly, the cop thought the **culprit** he had arrested was **culpable.**

cumbersome (adjective): awkward due to large size. "KUM bir some"

Think: **cucumber.**

It felt **cumbersome** to walk down the beach with a gigantic **cucumber** down the front of my Speedo.

cunning (adjective): cleverly forethought, often in a tricky or deceptive way. "KUN ing"

Think: **cunning kung-fu**.

In my opinion, the best kind of kung-fu is **cunning kung-fu**, where you seek to defeat your opponent through **deception** instead of just physical skill.

cupidity (noun): greedy desire for. "cue PID it ee"

Think: **Cupid**.

After being shot by **Cupid's** arrow, Sarah developed such **cupidity** for her valentine that she called him daily.

curmudgeon (noun): a grumpy old man. "kur MUDGE in"

Think: **curse mud**.

Only a **curmudgeon** would **curse** the **mud** in the garden on this sunny spring day.

cursory (adjective): hasty; superficial. "CURSE uh ree"

Think: **curse sorry**.

I only gave my rental car a **cursory** inspection, which led me to **curse** and be **sorry** later when I noticed a huge dent.

curtail (verb): to lessen. "kur TAIL"

Think: **cut** off your **tail**.

If you really want to win this lizard beauty pageant, you've got to be shorter. **curtail** your length - **cut** off your **tail**.

cynical (adjective): believing that people are generally selfish and dishonest. "SIN ick ull"

Think: **sin ick.**

I used to be optimistic, but now that I'm older and more **cynical**, I expect that, given the chance, most people will take whatever they want even if they have to **sin. Ick!**

cynosure (noun): something that guides or stands out. "SINE uh sure"

Think: **sign** to be **sure**.

Polaris (the North Star) was a **cynosure** for ancient sailors, a **sign** they could be **sure** of.

daunt (verb): to intimidate or discourage. "DAUNT"

Think: **don't!**

My mean old aunt Mildred would often **daunt** me when I was younger by screaming, "**don't!**" whenever I got too loud.

dearth (noun): lack. "DEARTH"

Think: **dead earth**.

Due to the **dead earth** of our farmland, there will be a **dearth** of food this winter.

debacle (noun): a complete disaster. "duh BAHK ul"

Think: **da bottle**.

I'm an alcoholic, so when I hit **da bottle**, the night usually becomes a **debacle**.

debased (adjective): lowered in value or reputation. "dee BASED"

Think: **de-base.**

Milk chocolate is a crime against the cacao bean. Confectioners start off with a **base** of pure dark chocolate, but then they **debase** it by adding milk powder and tons of sugar.

debauchery (noun): extreme indulgence in pleasure. "duh BOTCH er ee"

Think: **the bachelor party**.

During **the bachelor party**, the wolf pack in The Hangover participated in some serious **debauchery**.

debilitate (verb): to weaken. "duh BILL it ate"

Think: **decrease ability**.

Cancer will often **debilitate** its victims and can **decrease** their **ability** to be active.

decadent (adjective): decaying; self-indulgent. "DEK uh dent"

Think: **decayed**.

In *WALL-E*, the **decadent** passengers of the spaceship have **decayed** into overweight, lazy, passive lumps.

decimate (verb): to destroy a large part of. "DESS uh mate"

Think: **decimal remains**.

At the start of our campaign, all of our soldiers were healthy, but attacks and disease have **decimated** the ranks so that only a **decimal remains** alive.

declaimed (verb): spoke loudly and self-importantly. "dee CLAIMED"

Think: **"I declare!"**

"Well, **I declare!**" the Southern belle **declaimed**.

decorous (adjective): well-behaved. "DECK or us"

Think: **the chorus**.

Kids in **the chorus** are usually not rebels - they're often **decorous**.

decrepit (adjective): worn-out; run-down. "duh CREP it"

Think: **scrap it**.

Your **decrepit** old car looks like crap; you should **scrap it**.

decried (verb): expressed strong disapproval about. "duh CRIED"

Think: **cried**.

After my boss **decried** my work in front of everyone, I went home and **cried**.

defamatory (adjective): something that hurts someone's reputation. "duh FAM ih tory"

Think: **de-fame**.

The **defamatory** Enquirer story will "**de-fame**" that actor; he'll lose his fame.

defenestrate (verb): to quickly throw out. "duh FEN eh strate"

Think: **defense demonstrate**.

If you **defenestrate** a burglar through a plate-glass window, your home **defense** is **demonstrated**.

defunct (adjective): no longer existing. "duh FUNKED"

Think: **de-function**.

When I can fly in my dreams, the law of gravity seems to be **defunct**, like it has been **"de-functioned"**.

degenerate (verb, adjective) verb: to move backward or decay, adjective: decayed. "duh JENN er it"

Think: **Jenner ate my dust**.

1976 Olympic decathlon champion Caitlyn **Jenner ate my dust** when I challenged her to a footrace; I guess that her speed has **degenerated** with age.

delectable (adjective): delightful; delicious.
"duh LECT uh bull"

Think: **delicious electable**.

Ryan Gosling should run for president since most women think he's **delectable** and **delicious** enough to be **electable**.

deleterious (adjective): harmful. "duh luh TEER ee us"

Think: **deletes**.

Using that old computer could be **deleterious** to your grade since it randomly **deletes** files.

delimit (verb): to determine the limit, boundary or extent of something. "dee LIM it"

Think: **determine limit.**

Partying until 3 am with your friends is a great way to **determine** your **limits**, but the next-morning hangover might lead you **delimit** your alcohol intake the next time you go out.

delineate (verb): to outline; to describe in detail.
"Dee LIN ee ate"

Think: **the line.**

The strip of masking tape I put down is **the line** that clearly **delineates** the two halves of this dorm room - keep your stuff on your side!

demagogue (noun): a leader who gains power by trickery.
"dem a GOG"

Think: **demigod.**

The cult was led by a **demagogue**; he manipulated followers into thinking he was a **demigod.**

demarcate (verb): to define; to set apart. "de MARK ate"

Think: **mark it.**

If you want to **demarcate** your side of the dorm room, **mark it** with a long piece of masking tape.

demean (verb): to lower in character, status, or reputation. "dee MEAN"

Think: **mean**.

Thanks to the jocks' **demeaning** comments to him, the new kid went home after his first day at our school and told his mom that we're all **mean**.

demeanor (noun): one's appearance and behavior. "duh ME ner"

Think: **meaner personality**.

Not only has my ambition diminished with age, but so has my **demeanor**: I used to have a **meaner personality**.

demotic (adjective): popular; common. "duh MOTT ick"

Think: **democratic**.

Obama uses **demotic** language in his speeches to seem more **democratic**.

demur (verb): to object. "duh MURE"

Think: **murmur**.

Though no one has spoken up yet, the **murmur** from the class suggests they **demur** to my idea that they do more homework.

denigrate (verb): to attack the reputation of or to put down. "DEN ih grate"

Think: **deny I'm great**.

If you **deny I'm great**, you **denigrate** me.

denizen (noun): inhabitant; one who is often at a place. "DEN uh zen"

Think: **den citizen**.

One of the **denizens** of the caves in my woods is a black bear - he's a bear **den citizen**.

denuded (verb): stripped bare. "duh NOOD id"

Think: **nude**.

Loggers **denuded** the forested rise, felling trees and trampling undergrowth until it was just an **nude** hill of earth.

depiction (noun): a representation. "Dee PICK shun"

Think: **the picture.**

The picture I drew of myself in kindergarten was a crude **depiction** of a human being: my self-portrait had no torso.

deplete (verb): to use up. "duh PLEET"

Think: **delete**.

Depleted uranium has had some of its radioactivity **deleted**.

deplore (verb): to hate.
"duh PLORE (rhymes with "floor")"

Think: **deep lore**.

I **deplore** (hate) when my uncle likes to tell that campfire ghost story like it's part of some **deep lore** that goes back generations: the truth is that he's just repeating the plot of his favorite horror movie.

depredate (verb): to take by force; to ravage; to ruin. "DEH pruh date"

Think: **predator**.

The **predators** in the forest will **depredate** your village's livestock if you don't build a really good fence and get guard dogs.

deride (verb): to make fun of. "duh RIDE"

Think: **Dee's ride**.

We all **deride Dee's ride** - it's a brown 1987 Buick with ghetto rims.

derivative (adjective): lacking originality.
"duh RIH vuh tiv"

Think: **derivative relatives**.

My father likes to claim that his recipes are unique, but the truth is that he learned everything he knows about cooking from Aunt Jean. In other words, his recipes are **derivative** of his **relative**.

descry (verb): to catch sight of; to discover. "dih SCRY"

Think: **describe**.

Ok, now that I **descry** the iceberg that we're sailing towards, I can **describe** it to you.

desecrate (verb): to violate something sacred.
"DEH suh krate"

Think: **de-sacred**.

If you peed on an altar, you would **desecrate** it, or "**de-sacred**" it - it would no longer be sacred.

desiccated (adjective): dried out. "DEH si kate id"

Think: **desert sick**.

The **desert** made me **sick** because the dry heat **desiccated** my body.

despoiled (verb): stripped of value. "duh SPOILED"

Think: **spoiled**.

Desperate for oil, the U.S. drilled in Alaska and **despoiled** the land, and act which **spoiled** it for future generations.

despot (noun): an all-powerful ruler. "DES put"

Think: **despicable**.

History has shown us that **despots** - like Kim Jong Il -are often **despicable** human beings.

desuetude (noun): disuse. "DES wuh tude"

Think: **disuse attitude**.

The unnecessary security guard at the knitting store had an air of lazy **desuetude** about him - kind of a **disuse attitude**.

deteriorate (verb): to worsen over time.
"duh TIER ee or eight"

Think: **the terrier ate**.

He's really cute, but **the terrier ate** all the sofa cushions while we were gone – he's really making our decor **deteriorate**!

devoid (adjective): completely lacking. "duh VOID"

Think: **the void**.

The void of deep space is **devoid** of air, warmth, or life.

devolve (verb): to become less advanced over time.
"duh VAHLV"

Think: **the Volvo**.

When I bought **the Volvo** in 1988, it was state-of-the-art, but since then it has slowly **devolved** into a hunk of junk.

devout (adjective): deeply religious or loyal.
"duh VOUT (rhymes with "out")"

Think: **devote**.

I'd say I'm **devout** – I have **devoted** my entire life to studying the bible.

dexterity (adjective): skill; good coordination.
"dex TERR it ee"

Think: **Dexter**.

The fictional serial killer **Dexter** has a grisly **dexterity** about the way he kills people.

diabolical (adjective): devilish. "dia BALL ih cull"

Think: **die abolish**.

Your law that makes cigarettes part of school lunches is **diabolical** and will cause children to **die**... **abolish** it!

diaphanous (adjective): so flimsy as to be see-through. "die APH in us"

Think: **Diana's fan**.

Princess **Diana's** delicate rice-paper **fan** was **diaphanous**.

diatribe (noun): an angry speech. "DIE a tribe"

Think: **die tribe**.

I didn't understand the words of his **diatribe**, but I guessed the native said I'd **die** from his **tribe** killing me.

dichotomy (noun): two-part, polarity, contrast. "die KOTT uh me"

Think: **Thy cot, oh my**.

Thy cot, oh my – it's so comfortable when I'm sleeping in it, but my back hurts so much when I get up.

didactic (adjective): designed to teach. "die DAKT ick"

Think: **dictionary tactic**.

The definitions in a **dictionary** use the **tactic** of explaining words clearly in order to be **didactic**.

diffident (adjective): timid. "DIFF uh dent"

Think: **difficult dentures**.

I'm **diffident** when in public because I'm self-conscious about how weird my **difficult dentures** look.

digression (noun): a departure from the main topic. "duh GRESH in"

Think: **Dig Russians**.

"Have I ever mentioned to you that I **dig White Russians**?" said Lebowski, trying to **change the subject** when confronted about Bunny's failed rescue.

dilatory (adjective): tending to procrastinate. "DILL a tor ee"

Think: **delay later.**

The **dilatory** gator liked to **delay** things until **later.**

dilettante (noun): a dabbler; one with superficial knowledge of an area. "DILL uh taunt"

Think: **diluted.**

The **dilettante's** knowledge of the subject was, understandably, **diluted.**

dilute (verb): to lessen the concentration of. "duh LOOT"

Think: **dilution is the solution.**

If your drink is too strong, then **dilution is the solution**: just add ice!

dint (noun): force; power. "DINT"

Think: Hulk's **dent.**

The Incredible Hulk made a **dent** in the car by **dint** of his enormous strength.

dire (adjective): desparate.
"DAHYER (rhymes with "fire")"

Think: **die**.

If you are afraid that you might **die**, then the situation is **dire**.

discomfit (verb): to embarrass or confuse. "dis KUM fit"

Think: **discomfort**.

Realizing one's suit had been replaced with a too-tight Speedo would **discomfort** and **discomfit** anyone.

disconcert (verb): to confuse or frustrate. "dis KUN sirt"

Think: **diss** the **concert**.

To liven up recitals, I **disconcert** the musicians by **dissing** the **concert**.

discreet (adjective): having or showing self-restraint and good judgment. "dis KREET"

Think: **this secrET**.

I'm pregnant - but please, be **discreET** and keep **this secrET** - if my parents find out, they'll kill me.

discrepancy (noun): a difference, divergence, or disagreement. "dis KREP in see"

Think: **this crepe vs. Nancy's.**

There seems to be a large **discrepancy** between the size **this crepe** of mine and that of Nancy's... I wonder whether she took a bite of mine while I wasn't looking.

discrete (adjective): individually distinct; separate. "dis KREET"

Think: **Crete.**

The Greek island of **Crete** is **discrete** because it doesn't touch any other land.

discriminate (verb): to notice subtle variations. "dis KRIM in ate"

Think: one meaning is criminal; one is neutral.

Discriminate (verb), so you'll know when "**discriminate**" is about prejudice and when it's about noticing.

disgruntled (adjective): displeased. "dis GRUNT ulled"

Think: **grunted.**

The fat warthog **grunted** to show he was **disgruntled** with his small dinner.

dismantle (verb): to take apart or destroy. "Dis MAN till"

Think: **Mickey Mantle.**

A 16-time baseball All-Star, **Mickey Mantle** often **dismantled** opposing teams with his brilliant hitting.

dismissive (adjective): showing rejection and contempt for. "dis MISS ive"

Think: **dismiss.**

When she sings "Call Me Maybe", Carly Rae Jepsen is **dismissive** because she **dismissed** all the other boys who tried to chase her.

disparage (verb): to insult or put down. "dis PARRIAGE (rhymes with "marriage")

Think: **despair** and **rage.**

He felt **despair** and **rage** because the rapper liked to diss and **disparage** him.

disparate (adjective): distinct; different. "DISS per it"

Think: **This parrot vs. that pirate.**

This parrot is **disparate** (different) from **that pirate** on whose shoulder it is sitting. They are **disparate** species, after all...even if they do look a bit alike.

dispassionate (adjective): not passionate / interested. "diss PASH in it"

Think: **not passionate.**

Dis = not, so **dispassionate** = not passionate (not interested).

dispatch (noun): speed; efficiency. "DIS patch"

Think: **dispatcher.**

If you want a job as a **dispatcher** - using the radio to direct police - you'd better have **dispatch.**

displacing (verb): removing from the usual place. "Dis place"

Think: **dis place to dat place.**

Don't think of your demotion as me **displacing** you - I'm just moving your desk from **dis place to dat place.**

disputatious (adjective): inclined to argue.
"dis pyoo TAY shus"

Think: **dispute**.

After being pulled over, the **disputatious** lawyer unwisely **disputed** the accuracy of the cop's radar gun.

dissemble (verb): to mislead, hide or conceal.
"dis EM bull"

Think: **disassemble** gun.

The terrorist tried to **dissemble** his plan by **disassembling** his gun before trying to smuggle it through airport security.

disseminated (verb): spread out. "dis EM in nate id"

Think: **diss 'em, Nate**.

His dad advised to "**diss 'em, Nate**", so Nate **disseminated** flyers all over the school that criticized his opponents in the election.

distension (noun): swelling. "dis TEN shun"

Think: **dis-tension**.

A belly showing **distension** after a huge meal might be because the person has weak abs with no muscle **tension**.

dither (verb): to stress out from indecision. "DITH ur"

Think: **ditz do either**.

You're such a **ditz** – you'd **do either** and it's making you **dither**.

diurnal (adjective): daily; of the daytime. "die URN ul"

Think: The **urinal**.

My use of the **urinal** is **diurnal** – I pee every day.

divergent (adjective): moving in different directions. "duh VERJE int"

Think: **Two roads diverged**.

"Two roads **diverged** in a yellow wood," begins the famous Robert Frost Poem, "The Road Not Taken."

divisive (adjective): creating disunity. "di VIE sive"

Think: **divide**.

Yoko Ono had a **divisive** effect on The Beatles, **dividing** the group into two parts.

docile (adjective): Calm, even-tempered. "DOSS ill"

Think: **doctor.**

The **docile doctor** remained calm even though his patient was clinging to life by a thread.

doctrinaire (noun): rigid and dogmatic. "DOCK trih NAIR (rhymes with "hair")"

Think: **Doctorate in Air.**

I once met an academic with a **Doctorate** (Ph.D) **in Air,** and I asked him whether oxygen molecules always travel in pairs. "Yes, they do," he said, "...with zero exceptions."

doggedness (noun): stubborn determination. "DOG ed ness"

Think: **dog-ness.**

The fighter's **doggedness**, even after he was knocked down, was like that of a fearless **Bulldog.**

doggerel (noun): poorly written verse. "DOG ur ul"

Think: **dog verse.**

Most Valentine's Day card poems are such **doggerel** that it seems as though **dogs** wrote the **verse.**

dogmatic (adjective): stubborn; inflexible. "dog MATICK"

Think: **dog** bath.

My **dog automatically** becomes **dogmatic** if you try to give him a bath, since he hates water.

dolorous (adjective): sad; mournful. "DOLL ur us"

Think: **Dolores's doldrums.**

I'd be **dolorous** and in the **doldrums** too if my name were **Dolores**.

dormant (adjective): temporarily inactive. "DOOR munt"

Think: **doorman.**

If you work as a **doorman**, you know that most of the time you're just standing there, **dormant**.

dour (adjective): gloomy; stern. "DOUR"

Think: **sour.**

The teacher's **dour** expression made her pupils feel **sour**.

draconian (adjective): cruelly strict. "druh KONY en"

Think: **Draco** Malfoy.

If **Draco** Malfoy had taught the Gryffindor students, I'm sure he would have been a **draconian** instructor.

droll (adjective): funny. "DROLL"

Think: **roll** (with laughter).

Droll humor makes me **roll** with laughter.

dubious (adjective): doubtful. "DOO bee us"

Think: **dubious doob.**

That is a **dubious doob**, my friend – it looks like oregano if you ask me.

dudgeon (noun): a tantrum caused by being offended. "DUDGE in"

Think: **dungeon grudge.**

I was in high **dudgeon** after they threw me in the **dungeon** for jaywalking, and I held a **grudge.**

dupe (verb): to trick. "DOOP"

Think: **dope**.

A **dope** is easy to **dupe**.

duplicitous (adjective): deceptive. "due PLISS it us"

Think: **duplicate-ness**.

Politicians try to make everyone like them, but their two-faced **duplicate-ness** is **duplicitous**.

dwindle (verb): to gradually become smaller. "DWIN dull"

Think: **candle**.

Our excitement at exploring the cave quickly turned to fear when we saw that our **candle** had burned low, **dwindling** into a stub that wouldn't last for long.

dyspeptic (adjective): grumpy. "diss PEP tick"

Think: **Pepto-Bismol**.

This **Pepto-Bismol** will prevent indigestion and the resulting **dyspeptic** mood.

ebullient (adjective): excitedly enthusiastic.
"uh BOOL ee int"

Think: **Red Bull**.

After I chugged a giant **Red Bull**, I felt extremely **ebullient**.

eclectic (adjective): varied. "ek LEK tick"

Think: **selection collection**.

If your musical tastes are **eclectic**, I can probably name any style **selection** and you'll say it's in your **collection**.

effaced (verb): made less visible. "uh FACED"

Think: **erased**.

On old nickels, Thomas Jefferson's face is often **effaced** to the point of almost being **erased**.

effete (adjective): without strength or vitality; weak; soft. "uh FET"

Think: **feeble**.

The former athlete became **effete** and **feeble** from years of just sitting on the couch.

efficacious (adjective): effective.
"eff ick A (sounds like the letter) shus"

Think: **effectiveness**.

If you have senioritis, a brief vacation is an **efficacious** way to increase your **effectiveness**.

efflorescence (noun): blossoming. "eff lerr REH since"

Think: **florist**.

Efflorescence is all around me – I'm a **florist**.

effluvium (noun): an invisible, often harmful, vapor. "uh FLOOVE lee um"

Think: **flu**.

The **effluvium** coming from the **flu** patient's mouth infected the nurse.

effrontery (noun): shameless boldness. "uh FRONT ur ree"

Think: **fronting homies**.

What's with these **homies** dissin' my girl? Why do they gotta **front**? (Because they have **effrontery**, Weezer.)

effusive (adjective): extremely expressive.
"uh FYUSE ive"

Think: **fussy**.

Imagine if Nicki Minaj was your grandma? She's so **effusive** she'd make a **fuss** over your every accomplishment.

egalitarian (adjective): based on the belief in human equality. "ee gal ih TAIR ee in"

Think: **equal eagle**.

In the U.S., our **egalitarian** belief that all men are created **equal** is symbolized by the bald **eagle**.

egregious (adjective): bad in an obvious way.
"uh GREE jis"

Think: **outrageous**.

Her saying that she had to wash her hamster was such an **egregious** and **outrageous** excuse that it made me say "Jesus!"

eldritch (adjective): weird; eerie. "el DRISH"

Think: **elf-witch**.

The **elf-witch** Galadriel in The Lord Of The Rings was **eldritch** because of her ability to speak inside our heads.

emancipate (verb): to free. "eh MAN sih payt"

Think: **Emancipation Proclamation**.

President Abraham Lincoln issued the **Emancipation Proclamation** on January 1, 1863. It declared "that all persons held as slaves" within the rebellious states "are, and henceforward shall be **free**."

embellish (verb): to decorate. "em BELL ish"

Think: **bells**.

Hanging little **bells** all over your home is one (weird) way to **embellish** it.

embroiled (verb): in a difficult situation. "em BROY uled"

Think: **on broil**.

I was **embroiled** in a dangerous situation when I got locked in an oven set **on "broil"**.

embryonic (adjective): in an early stage. "em bree ON ick"

Think: **embryo**.

It's pretty obvious that a human **embryo** is **embryonic** when compared to an adult human.

eminent (adjective): respected, famous, well-known. "EM ih nint"

Think: **Eminem**.

If asked to name the most **eminent** white rapper, I wouldn't think twice: **Eminem** is an easy choice. (Sorry Macklemore.)

emollient (adjective): soothing. "uh MOLE ee int"

Think: **emo**.

Listening to **emo** music has an **emollient** effect on my emotions because it's so sensitive.

emphatic (adjective): forceful. "em FAT ick"

Think: **emphasize**.

When I yell at people, I **emphasize** every word to be more **emphatic** about my demands.

empirical (adjective): observed, firsthand.
"em PEER ih cuhl"

Think: **miracle**.

If you're claiming that there was a **miracle** here, then I would like to see some **empirical** evidence that it happened.

encomium (noun): praise. "en COH mi um"

Think: **in Comic-Con**.

In Comic-Con, the entertainment convention, nerds give **encomium** to the latest comic-book movies.

encompass (verb): to include. "en KUM pess"

Think: **compass**.

Use this **compass** to draw a circle around the things you want to **encompass**.

encroaching (verb): gradually invading one's rights or property. "en KROACH ing"

Think: **roaches**.

My apartment's **roaches** are **encroaching** upon my space: they now occupy the kitchen.

enervating (adjective): tiring. "EN ur vating"

Think: **renovating.**

Renovating their kitchen by themselves not only got on the couple's nerves, but also was extremely **enervating**.

enigmatic (adjective): mysterious, unpredictable. "en igg MAT ick"

Think: **dark matter.**

Dark matter comprises most of the universe but remains **enigmatic** to scientists.

enmity (noun): hatred. "EN mit ee"

Think: **enemy.**

I have **enmity** for my **enemy** - what else would you expect?

ennui (noun): dissatisfaction resulting from boredom. "ON we"

Think: **ennui there yet?**

Take a seven-year-old on a long car ride, and you'll hear the **ennui** in his voice when he repeatedly asks, "**ennui there yet**?"

ensorcelled (adjective): bewitched; enchanted. "EN sir celled"

Think: **sorcerer**.

The **sorcerer ensorcelled** the adventurers with a powerful spell that made them forget who they were.

entitled (adjective): pompous, conceited. "en TIGHT ild"

Think: **N possible titles**.

If your name begins with "Count," "Duke," "Prince" or any other of **N possible titles**, then you're probably **entitled**.

entreat (verb): to plead. "en TREAT"

Think: **in retreat**.

In retreat, the fleeing general **entreated** us to spare his soldiers' lives.

ephemeral (adjective): fleeting; short-lived. "Eh FEM er ul"

Think: **FM for all**.

Since satellite radio is ten times better than normal radio, the days of **FM for all** are **ephemeral**.

epitome: adjective, the purest or best example of something. "uh PIT uh me"

Think: **epic tome**

When it comes to classic literature, "Moby Dick" is the **epitome** of an **epic tome**.

equivocal (adjective): intentionally unclear. "uh QUIV oh cull"

Think: **equally vocal**.

The **equivocal** politician was **equally vocal** about both sides of the issue.

eradicate (verb): to wipe out. "ee RAD ih kate"

Think: **radiate**.

You can **radiate** food to **eradicate** the bacteria in it.

ersatz (adjective): being an artificial and inferior substitute. "AIR sotts"

Think: **Er, Saltz?**

When I tried using **Saltz** by Pfitzer (TM) instead of actual table **salt**, I found it to be an **inferior substitute**.

erstwhile (adjective): former. "ERST while"

Think: **Hearse after a while.**

It's important to prepare for the future, but also to live for the moment. One must remember that our lives will eventually become our **erstwhile** lives, because we're all destined for the **hearse after a while**.

erudite (adjective): knowledgeable (from studying). "ERR ooh dite"

Think: **he read it.**

My English professor is so **erudite**: every time I bring up a great book I don't think he knows about, it turns out that **he read it**.

eschew (verb): to avoid. "us CHOO"

Think: **ah-choo!**

Eschew people who say "**ah-choo!**" unless you want to catch their colds.

esoteric (adjective): known by only a few people. "ess oh TERR (rhymes with "err") ick"

Think: **isolated terrific**.

Einstein's **esoteric** knowledge **isolated** him from most of his peers since his acumen was so **terrific**.

espouse (verb): to support or to give loyalty to. "ess POUZE"

Think: **spouse**.

Chances are that you will **espouse** your **spouse** - you married her, so you probably have her back.

espy (verb): to glimpse; to catch sight of. "uh SPY"

Think: **I spy**.

I spy something blue - do you **espy** it, too?

estimable (adjective): worthy. "ESS tim uh ble"

Think: **esteem-able**.

If someone is **estimable** they are **"esteem-able"**, i.e., they're deserving of your positive regard.

estranged (verb): separated in a negative way.
"uh STRANGED"

Think: **stranger**.

Gotye's **estranged** girlfriend cut him out and treated him like a **stranger** and it felt so rough.

ethereal (adjective): delicate; heavenly; insubstantial.
"uh THEER ee ul"

Think: **other** than **real**.

My God, Joyce - your meringue cookies are **ethereal** - so light, so delicious - they must be something **other** than **real**.

etiolated (verb): made pale; weakened. "EE tea uh late id"

Think: **toilet-ed**.

Keeping my goldfish in the bleach-containing **toilet** tank violated his trust and **etiolated** him so much that he turned white.

euphemism (noun): an inoffensive term used in place of an offensive one. "YOOF ih mism"

Think: **use feminism**.

Use feminism if you're a guy and want to create a **euphemism** for PMS – otherwise you might get yourself killed.

eurytopic (adjective): tolerant of many different environments. "you ree TOP ick"

Think: **Europe tropics**.

That plant is **eurytopic** because it grows both in cold, rainy **Europe** and in the hot, humid **tropics**.

evanescent (adjective): fleeting; lasting only briefly. "eh van ESS sint"

Think: **vanish scent**.

The cologne's fragrance will **vanish** soon; its **scent** is **evanescent**.

evinced (verb): revealed. "uh VINSED"

Think: **evidence**.

Vince **evinced** the villain by providing **evidence**.

exacerbated (verb): made more severe; aggravated. "eggs ZASS er bait id"

Think: **exasperated**.

I'm **exasperated** - not only did you get us lost in the woods, but you also **exacerbated** the situation by dropping our phone in that swamp.

exact (verb): to take. "egg ZACKT"

Think: **Exacto knife**.

I'm going to **exact** my share of the cookie with an **Exacto** knife.

exacting (adjective): requiring strict attention to detail. "egg ZAKT ing"

Think: **exact**.

Our **exacting** architecture professor demanded that our model be drawn **exactly** to scale.

exaggerate (verb): to overestimate or underestimate, stretch the truth or hyperbolize. "eks ADGE urr ate"

Think: **ex's age rate.**

My **ex** likes to **exaggerate** his **age rate** in the reverse direction: last year he told people he was 39, but now he's claiming that he's 38.

excise (verb): to take or cut out. "eck SIZE"

Think: **ex-size.**

During liposuction, doctors **excise** fat – your current size will be an **ex-size** and you'll be skinny.

excoriated (verb): strongly condemned.
"ex KOR ee ate id"

Think: **scoured.**

Simon Cowell's criticism on American Idol **excoriated** the contestant – she felt as if she'd been **scoured** by a rough dish pad.

exculpated (verb): freed from blame. "ex CULL pate id"

Think: **ex-culprit.**

If you commit a crime but have a clever lawyer, you'll be **exculpated** and be an "**ex-culprit**".

execrable (adjective): detestable; awful.
"ex eh CRUH bull"

Think: **excrement**.

Your unfunny jokes about **excrement** are **execrable** –
they're shit.

exigent (adjective): requiring immediate and/or significant
action. "EX ih gent"

Think: **exit gent.**

When there's an **exigent** problem, Clark Kent becomes an
exit gent and returns as Superman.

exodus (noun): the departure of many people.
"EX uh duss"

Think: **exit us!**

During the Syrian civil war, there was a mass **exodus** of
refugees who must have been thinking, "**exit us!**"

exorbitant (adjective): excessive. "ex ORB it int"

Think: **extra** for **orbit**.

The fancy space hotel charged **exorbitant** fees due to the
extra costs needed to **orbit** the earth.

expatiate (verb): to speak or write about in detail.
"ex PAY she ate"

Think: **paid she ate = food critic.**

Sarah loved to eat and to write, so she decided that she watned to **expatiate** as a food critic and get **paid** when **she ate.**

expatriate (noun): one who has moved to a foreign country. "ex PAY tree ate"

Think: **ex-patriot.**

We said our **expatriate** friend was an anti-American **ex-patriot** since he moved to France.

expedient (adjective): helpful in a practical way.
"ex PEED ee int"

Think: **speedy.**

To be **speedy,** I booked my flight on Expedia.com; it was more **expedient** than calling the airline.

explicate (verb): to explain, analyze, or develop an idea.
"EX plih kate"

Think: **looks like "explain".**

To **explain** is to make explicit, or **explicate.**

exponent (noun): a supporter of something. "EX poe nint"

Think: **ex-opponent**.

Upon Romney's nomination, McCain became his **exponent** for the greater good of the GOP and therefore was his **ex-opponent**.

expunge (verb): to get rid of. "ex PUNJ"

Think: **ex** with **sponge**.

The best way to make a spill an "**ex**-spill" is to use a **sponge** to **expunge** the mess.

expurgate (verb): to cleanse. "EX per gate"

Think: **purge**.

By the time they were done **expurgating** the "offensive" parts from *Huckleberry Finn*, there was almost nothing left; they **purged** almost everything.

extant (adjective): present or existing (opposite of extinct). "EX tint"

Think: **existing ant**.

Since he was about to get stepped on, "I **exist**!" exclaimed the **ant** to the elephant.

extemporaneous (adjective): done without preparation. "ex tem per RAIN ee us"

Think: **ex= without, tempo= time**.

If you don't have time to prepare, then your speech will have to be **extemporaneous**.

extenuating (adjective): less serious due to a partial excuse. "ex TEN you ate ing"

Think: **extension**.

I got an **extension** on my paper because there were **extenuating** circumstances – I got trampled by an elephant.

extirpate (verb): to get rid of completely. "EK stir pate"

Think: **exterminate**.

If you have pests in your house that you want to **extirpate**, call someone who will **exterminate** them.

extol (verb): to praise highly. "ek STOLL"

Think: **ex-toll**.

I **extol** this highway because it used to charge a toll, but now it's an **ex-toll** road.

extraneous (adjective): not important. "eks TRAIN ee us"

Think: **extra strain.**

Just give me the facts, ma'am. All these **extraneous** details are putting an **extra strain** on my memory.

extrapolate (verb) to infer, conclude or draw a conclusion based on another observation or fact. "eks TRAP oh late"

Think: **Extra police = we'll be late**

Due to the fact that there are **extra police** on the highway today, and traffic is at a standstill, I'm guessing that there was a big accident. Hence, I can **extrapolate** that **we'll be late** to work today.

exult: verb, to show great happiness. "eggs ult"

Think: **ultimate ex**

I **exulted** in the fact that my **ex** still plays **ultimate** Frisbee with me, since **ultimate** has always been my one true love.

fabricate (verb): to make up in order to deceive.
"FAB rick ate"

Think: **fabric** background.

The movie set background was **fabricated**, woven from **fabric** to resemble a mountain range.

facetious (adjective): playfully funny. "fa SEE shus"

Think: **face "E".**

The **facetious** comedian made us smile so much that our **faces** looked like we were constantly saying **"E".** (try it!)

fallible (adjective): capable of making an error. "FAL (rhymes with "pal") ih bull"

Think: **fail-able.**

Jenkins! The rookie agent you picked is **fallible** – for him, the mission is extremely **fail-able.**

fanatic (adjective): full of extreme enthusiasm. "fuh NAT ick"

Think: **fan lunatic.**

The **fanatic** Green Bay Packers **fan** - a **lunatic** - painted his face green and wore a cheesehead hat every day of the year.

farce (noun): a comical, unrealistic, mocking display or show. "FARSE"

Think: **farts.**

I know your play is a **farce** because of how many times the characters **fart.**

fastidious (adjective): having very picky standards. "fuh STID ee us"

Think: **fast to tidy up**.

My roommate is **fastidious** about cleaning; she gets mad if I am not **fast to tidy up** the apartment.

fatuous (adjective): lazily foolish. "fat SHOE us"

Think: **fat ass**.

If you're **fatuous** about nutrition, you might end up with a **fat ass**.

fawning (verb) kissing up to. "FON ing"

Think: **fawn** (baby deer).

The little **fawn's** only hope to get the bear to spare its life was by using **fawning** behavior.

feckless (adjective): weak; worthless; irresponsible. "FEK liss"

Think: **F** in **class**.

If you get an **F** in **class**, your study habits were probably **feckless**.

fecund (adjective): fruitful; inventive. "FEE kund"

Think: **feces under**.

Spreading manure, i.e., **feces**, **under** your crops as fertilizer will make your harvest **fecund**.

feign (verb): to fake. "FAYN (rhymes with "rain")"

Think: **faint**.

Here's the plan: we **feign** illness by pretending to **faint** as soon as the final exam begins so we won't have to take it.

felicity (noun): happiness. "fu LISS it ee"

Think: **feline city**.

If you're a cat person, then a **feline city** would bring you great **felicity**. Meow.

ferret (verb): to bring to light; to uncover. "FERR it"

Think: **ferret** (the animal).

If you keep a **ferret** as a pet, it will **ferret** out all your lost earrings since they can crawl under anything.

fervor (noun): passion. "FURR ver"

Think: **fever**.

The lovers' **fervor** for each other was so great that their skin felt **fever**-hot.

festoon (verb): to decorate. "feh STOON"

Think: **festival**.

The harvest moon **festival** is coming! Time to **festoon** the barn for the big dance!

fetid (adjective): bad-smelling. "FED id"

Think: **feet**.

Feet are often **fetid**.

fiasco (noun): a disaster. "fee ASS koh"

Think: **flask**.

Smuggling that **flask** into the football game was a **fiasco**; we got kicked out in the first quarter.

filial (adjective): like a son or daughter. "FIL ee ul"

Think: **affiliated**.

It was the son's **filial** duty to care for his dying mother since he was **affiliated** with her by blood.

fillip (noun): stimulus, impetus, flick. "PHIL ipp"

Think: **fill up my tank.**

If you could please **fill up** my tank of gas, then that would be a **fillip** to my transportation abilities.

finagled (verb): obtained, often through trickery or indirect methods. "fih NAY gulled"

Think: **finagle** a **bagel**.

Even though I had lost my wallet, I **finagled** a **bagel** from the bagel lady by claiming I had invented cream cheese.

finicky (adjective): difficult to please. "FIN ick ee"

Think: **nit-picky**.

The princess was **nit-picky** – she was so **finicky** that she refused to sleep on the mattress with a pea under it.

fitful (adjective): irregular; intermittent. "FIT full"

Think: **fit-full**.

Our new baby only sleeps **fitfully** – the night seems **full** of his crying **fits**.

flagrant (adjective): shockingly bad. "FLAY grint"

Think: **fragrant vagrant**.

No matter what your feelings towards homeless people are, you can't deny that man is a **fragrant vagrant** - his B.O. is so bad it's **flagrant**.

fleeting (adjective): short-lived. "FLEET ing"

Think: **flee**.

My stay in the village was by necessity **fleeting**: a dragon attacked, and I had to **flee**.

flippant (adjective): lacking respect or seriousness. "FLIP int"

Think: **flip off**.

If you're **flippant**, you probably **flip** people **off** on a regular basis.

florid (adjective): overly decorated; reddish. "FLOR id"

Think: **flowered**.

The 12-year-old girl's room was **flowered** with hundreds of red-hued decorations - her style was **florid**.

flotilla (noun): a fleet of ships. "flo TILL uh"

Think: **floating** around **Godzilla**.

Floating around **Godzilla** was a **flotilla** from the Japanese navy.

flotsam (noun): floating debris. "FLOT sim"

Think: **float**.

After the Titanic sank, Rose was able to survive by climbing onto a piece of **floating flotsam** from the wreckage.

flounder (verb): to act clumsily or ineffectively. "FLOUN dir"

Think: **flop under**.

Bad dancers **flounder** (verb) through clubs like flounders (noun) that **flop under** the seat of the boat once they're caught.

flourish (verb): to thrive. "FLERR ish"

Think: **florist**.

My flowers always **flourish**, because I have 20 years experience as a **florist**.

flouted (verb): treated without respect. "FLOUT id"

Think: **flung out**.

The rebel **flouted** the rules so badly that he **flung** them **out** the window.

fluctuate (verb): to change or go back and forth. "FLUCK chew ate"

Think: **flocked**.

Sometimes customers have **flocked** to our restaurant, and other times we are half empty: demand seems to **fluctuate**.

flummoxed (adjective): confused. "FLUM ixed"

Think: **flume ox**.

At the water park, I was completely **flummoxed** when, in the **flume** ride, I saw an **ox** swimming along.

foible (noun): a minor weakness of character. "FOY bull"

Think: **foil-able**.

Your plan to take over the world is **foil-able** because you have many **foibles**.

foment (verb): to encourage the growth of. "FOH ment"

Think: **form it!**

In *Star Wars*, Princess Leia **fomented** the Rebel group by telling the Rebels to "**form it!**"

forage (verb, noun) v: to search for food, n: food, a search. "FORE ige"

Think: **for aged cheese**.

Being French, I have been **foraging** our supermarkets and farmer's markets far and wide **for aged cheese** that reminds me of home.

forbearance (noun): patience; tolerance. "four BEAR ints"

Think: **bear tolerance**.

I'm usually harsh on people who borrow my money, but for **bears** I have more **tolerance** and practice **forbearance** since they scare me.

foreground (verb): to highlight. "FOUR ground"

Think: **foreground** (noun).

That boy is magic! **Foreground** (verb) his talent by making sure he's in the **foreground** (noun) of the stage!

forestall (verb): to delay, hinder, or prevent. "four STALL"

Think: **for stall**.

The booby traps I surrounded my fort with will **forestall** invaders – they're **for stalling**.

formidable (adjective): serious, respectable, worthy. "FOR mid ih bull"

Think: **forbid**.

The cliff face was **formidable**; it seemed to **forbid** us from even attempting to climb.

fortitude (noun): strength. "FORT ih tude"

Think: **fortress**.

The Bulgarian weightlifter's mental **fortitude** during training gave him a body that looked like a **fortress**.

fortuitous (adjective): lucky. "for TWO it iss"

Think: **fortunate** for **us**.

It was **fortuitous** and **fortunate** for **us** that the polar bear we encountered had just eaten a seal and was too full to eat us.

fracas (noun): a noisy brawl. "FRAH kiss"

Think: **frat ruckus**.

The **frat** brothers often caused a **ruckus** by getting into a drunken **fracas**.

fractious (adjective): cranky. "FRAK shis"

Think: **fracture us**.

The **fractious** football player is best avoided: if his team loses, he gets mad enough to **fracture us**.

fraternize (verb): to be friendly with. "FRAH turn eyes"

Think: **frat**.

We **frat** brothers **fraternize** with all the freshman chicks so they'll come to our parties.

frenetic (adjective): wildly excited or active.
"fruh NET ick"

Think: **frenzy** of **energy**.

Have you ever watched a Pug play? It's **frenetic** - like a chubby little **frenzy** of **energy**.

froward (adjective): stubbornly disobedient. "FRO werd"

Think: **afro**.

I try to straighten my hair but it's **froward** - after a few hours, it's a **fro** again.

frugal (adjective): thrifty; inclined to save money.
"FROO gull"

Think: **fructose** corn syrup **gal**.

I'm too **frugal** to use healthy sweeteners - I'm a high-**fructose** corn syrup **gal**.

fruition (noun): a productive result. "froo ISH un"

Think: grow **fruit**.

My plans to grow my own oranges came to **fruition** when my orange tree produced **fruit**.

fudge (verb): to fake or falsify. "FUDJ"

Think: **"oh, fudge!"**

If the salesperson **fudges** the facts about the used car you buy, you'll be saying **"oh, fudge!"** later when it breaks down.

fuliginous (adjective): obscure; murky; dark.
"few LIDGE in is"

Think: **full of gin**.

After he was **full of gin**, James Joyce composed poetry so moody and **fuliginous** that few could appreciate it.

fulsome (adjective): abundant, sometimes disgustingly so.
"FULL some"

Think: **full** of **some**.

In the U.S., we are **full** of **some** crops - for instance, corn here is so **fulsome** that we put it in nearly every food product.

funereal (adjective): like a funeral. "fyoo NERR ee ul"

Think: **funeral**.

Your gothic style is so **funereal** it looks as though you're headed to a **funeral** instead of the mall.

furor (noun): an outburst of rage or excitement. "FURE rir"

Think: **furious.**

The governor's use of the Fuhrer's (Hitler's) image in an ad made many **furious** and created a political **furor.**

furtive (adjective): done by stealth. "FIR tive"

Think: **furtive fart.**

Watch out for that kid - he will **fart** in class but it's so **furtive** that he never gets blamed.

gadfly (noun): someone who annoys by being very critical. "GAD fly"

Think: **egad, fly!**

Brad is such a **gadfly** about my outfits that I want to say "**Egad, fly!**" and hit him with a flyswatter.

gaffe (noun): a social mistake. "GAFF"

Think: **laugh.**

It's definitely a **gaffe** to bring your pet giraffe to the party - everyone will **laugh.**

gainsay (verb): to deny. "GAIN say"

Think: **against say**.

Those who **gainsay** us are **against** what we **say**.

gallant (adjective): courageous; noble. "GAL int"

Think: **galloping** knight.

She's still single because she's waiting for a **gallant** knight to come **galloping** in on his horse and sweep her away.

gambit (noun): a move made to try to gain an advantage. "GAM bit"

Think: **gamble it**.

When you play chess, sometimes you have to **gamble it** and use a **gambit** by sacrificing a piece for a better position.

gamboled (verb): danced around happily; frolicked. "GAM bulled"

Think: **game ball**.

After she scored three goals and led the team to victory, the coach awarded her the **game ball** and she **gamboled** all over the place.

garble (verb): to make hard to understand. "GAR bull"

Think: **gargle**.

A bad connection can **garble** a voicemail to the point that the message just sounds like someone mid-**gargle**.

gargantuan (adjective): enormous.
"gar (rhymes with "far") GAN shoo-in"

Think: **gigantic**.

The **gargantuan** orangutan was so **gigantic** that it needed a special enclosure at the zoo.

garrulous (adjective): talkative, chatty, prone to discussing trivial things. "GARE rule luss"

Think: **girls rule us**.

The reason those **girls rule us** is that they have a talent for being **garrulous** – we can barely get a word in during conversation.

gauche (adjective): awkward. "GOSH"

Think: **go douche**.

The **gauche** thing about Summer's Eve commercials is that they're basically telling you to **go douche**.

146

gaudy (adjective): flashy in a tasteless way. "GODDY"

Think: **gawd ugly**.

The rapper's inch-thick gold chain was so **gaudy** that even his fans said, "**gawd** that's **ugly**!"

genial (adjective): good-natured. "JEAN ee ul"

Think: **genie**.

If you sign up to be a **genie** and to grant people wishes, you're probably by nature **genial**.

germane (adjective): relevant; appropriate; fitting. "jer MAIN"

Think: **yer main.**

Enough digressions! Stick to **yer main** point; unless your remarks are **germane**, I get distracted.

germinate (verb): to grow or to cause to grow. "JERM in ate"

Think: **germ in Nate**.

After entering his nose, the **germ in Nate** was able to **germinate** into a cold because he was so run down.

ghastly (adjective): horrid. "GASSED lee"

Think: **ghostly**.

Looking in the mirror and seeing a **ghostly** figure behind me was **ghastly**.

gild (verb): to make attractive, often deceptively. "GILLED"

Think: **gold**.

I'm a terrible painter, so instead I usually **gild** my vases with **gold** so they look okay.

glacial (adjective): slow and/or cold. "GLAY shull"

Think: **glacier**.

My answer had a **glacial** (slow) pace, and the interviewer gave me a **glacial** (cold) look that made me feel like I was on a **glacier**.

glancing (adjective): indirect. "GLANSE ing"

Think: **glance** (verb).

The knight only **glanced** sideways at his opponent; as a result, his lance's blow was **glancing** and didn't inflict any damage.

148

glaring (adjective): obvious; harshly bright. "GLARE ing"

Think: **glare**.

My resume had such a **glaring** typo that my interviewer just sat there and **glared** at me until I left.

glowered (verb): looked at with anger. "GLAH werd"

Think: **glow RRR**.

The scary, frowning jack-o'-lantern **glowered** at us - its **glow** seemed to say "RRRRRRRR!"

glut (noun): too much of something. "GLUT"

Think: **glutton**.

Since my dog is a **glutton** for dog treats, I have a **glut** of Snausages in my house.

goosebumps (noun): small bumps on the skin caused by fear or excitement. "Goose bumps"

Think: **goose bumps.**

Pluck the feathers off the skin of a **goose**, and you'll see the same little **bumps** that appear on your forearms when you get scared.

gossamer (adjective): delicate; flimsy.
"GAWS a murr"

Think: **goose feather**.

Wafting through the air, the **goose feather** was **gossamer** and felt soft to the touch when it landed on my palm.

grandiloquent (adjective): loud; colorful; egotistical.
"gran DILL oh quent"

Think: **grand eloquent**.

If you're **grandiloquent**, you're **grand** and **eloquent** with your speech so everyone notices you.

grandiose (adjective): affecting grandness by showing off or exaggerating. "GRAN dee ose"

Think: **grand ideas**.

I have a lot of **grand ideas**: for example, my **grandiose** plan to jump the Grand Canyon with my rocket car.

grandstand (verb): to show off. "GRAND stand"

Think: **handstand**.

If you're doing a **handstand**, it's probably to **grandstand** for an audience.

grasping (adjective): excessively greedy. "GRASP ing"

Think: Mr. Burns' **grasping**.

The Simpsons' Mr. Burns is a **grasping** (adjective) tycoon who is always **grasping** (verb) at any new source of profit.

grating (adjective): irritating. "GREAT ing"

Think: **grater**.

Reading Facebook election posts is **grating**; I'd almost rather rub a cheese **grater** on myself.

gravitas (noun): powerful seriousness. "GROV it oss"

Think: **gravity**.

As the judge entered, his **gravitas** was like **gravity**, drawing everyone's eyes to him and silencing the room.

gregarious (adjective): social. "gruh GAIR ee us"

Think: **congregate**.

If you're **gregarious**, you like to **congregate** with others whenever possible.

grisly (adjective): horrific; disgusting. "GRIS lee"

Think: **grizzly** death.

If you piss off a **grizzly** bear, it may give you a **grisly** death.

grouse (verb): to complain.
"GRAHWSE (rhymes with "house")"

Think: **Grouch**.

Oscar the **Grouch** likes to **grouse** about everyone else on Sesame Street.

grovel (verb): to act like an unworthy servant by crawling or lowering oneself. "GRAH vuhl"

Think: **gravel**.

Grovel to Her Majesty by putting your face in the **gravel**, slave!

gumption (noun): drive; initiative. "GUMP shun"

Think: Forrest **Gump**.

Forrest **Gump** showed **gumption** by playing football, co-founding a shrimp business, and running across the country.

guttural (adjective): strange and unpleasant sounding. "GUT ur ul"

Think: **gutter roar**.

You'd have the **guttural gutter roar** of a homeless man if you spent the night sleeping in the gutter.

hackneyed (adjective): trite or overused. "HACK need"

Think: **hacked knees**.

The veteran soccer player had **hacked knees**; his knees were **hackneyed** from overuse.

haggard (adjective): worn-out looking. "HAH gerd"

Think: **hag**.

After months of partying with little sleep, Lindsay Lohan began to look **haggard** and worried people would think she was an old **hag**.

halcyon (adjective): happy; peaceful; prosperous. "HAL see yon"

Think: **hell's she on?**

In her **halcyon** years, people would ask "What the **hell's she on?**" because she was constantly happy.

hallowed (adjective): sacred. "HAL owed"

Think: **halo-ed**.

The cemetery where saints are buried is so **hallowed** it's practically "**halo-ed**".

hapless (adjective): unlucky. "HAP less"

Think: **happy less**.

The **hapless** are often **happy less** because of their rotten luck.

haptic (adjective): related to the sense of touch. "HAP tick"

Think: **half ticked**.

I am only **half ticked** off that my **haptic** senses are fading with age, since my resistance to pain has also increased.

harangue (noun): a ranting lecture. "huh RANG"

Think: **her ears rang**.

Her ears rang so much after the loud **harangue** that she joked she'd rather hang than listen to it again.

harbinger (noun): something that shows what will happen in the future. "har BINJ er"

Think: **bringer**.

The superstitious woman thought the black cat crossing her path was a **harbinger** of bad luck and a **bringer** of misfortune.

hardscrabble (adjective): involving struggle and hard work. "HARD skrab bull"

Think: **hard and scrappy scrabble champ**.

Despite her **hardscrabble** upbringing, Lucinda was a **hard and scrappy scrabble champ**; she excelled not because of her genius, but through **hard work** and a superior will to win.

harmonious (adjective): free from disagreement; forming a pleasing whole. "Har MOAN ee us"

Think: **harp money**.

Playing the **harp** brings me as much **money** as it does because the way I play is so **harmonious**.

harried (adjective): harassed.
"HAH (rhymes with "NAH") reed"

Think: **hurried**.

Being **harried** by your teacher and **hurried** to finish your test - just because you're the last one in the room - is terrible.

harrow (verb): to torment or greatly distress.
"HAH (rhymes with "NAH") rowed"

Think: **hair arrow**.

Not two days after I'd grown the perfect afro, my friend decided to **harrow** me by shooting me in the **hair** with an **arrow**.

haughty (adjective): proud in a way that looks down on others. "HOT ee"

Think: stuck-up **hottie**.

Unfortunately, that senior class **hottie** is usually **haughty** when you talk to her.

headlong (adjective): done without adequate thinking; rash. "HEAD long"

Think: **headfirst**.

If you dived **headfirst** into a shallow pool, it would be a **headlong** decision.

hector (verb): to bully or harass. "HEK tir"

Think: **heckle**.

I tried to **hector** the comedian by **heckling** him, but he made fun of me, so I stopped.

hegemony (noun): dominance. "HEJ uh moany"

Think: **huge money**.

The country with **huge** amounts of **money** enjoyed **hegemony** over its neighbors because it could afford an immense army.

heinous (adjective): wicked; hateable. "HAIN us"

Think: **anus**.

I called you an **anus** because of your **heinous** deeds – you cheated on me!

herald (noun, verb) n: messenger, indicator, omen v: to signal the arrival of. "HAIR uhld"

Think: **Harold the Herald**.

"**Harold the Herald**" would be a great name for a psychic who **heralds** the future... if people had more capacious vocabularies.

hermetic (adjective): protected from outside influence. "her MET ick"

Think: **hermit**.

The **hermit** lived in a **hermetic** cave that was only reachable via a treacherous mountain path.

heterodox (adjective): unorthodox; unconventional. "HETT er oh docks"

Think: **hetero = different**.

If you are heterosexual, then you prefer the opposite (**different**) sex. If you are **heterodox**, then you prefer an unconventional (**different**) lifestyle and/or philosophy.

heterogeneous (adjective): made of dissimilar parts. "heh te-ro JEAN ee-us"

Think: **heterosexual**.

Heterosexual sex is more **heterogeneous** than homosexual sex since it involves a wider variety of body parts.

heyday (noun): one's best time period. "HAY day"

Think: **hey day**.

During my **heyday**, when I was the starting quarterback and had a 4.0, all the girls said **hey** to me every **day**.

hiatus (noun): an interruption or break. "hi A (sounds like the letter A) tus"

Think: **Hyatt**.

The Hawaiian **Hyatt** ad urged us to take a **hiatus** from work to stay at its luxurious hotel for a few days.

hidebound (adjective): inflexible; ultra-conservative. "HIDE bound"

Think: **hide-bound**.

The **hidebound** extremists were **bound** in animal **hides** and unsurprisingly were against gay marriage.

hirsute (adjective): hairy. "her STOOT"

Think: **hair suit**.

I saw an old guy in the locker room who was so **hirsute** that he looked like he was wearing a **hair suit**.

histrionic (adjective): overly emotional for effect. "hiss tree ON ick"

Think: **hysterical**.

Her **hysterical** laughter was designed to get attention and was therefore **histrionic**.

hodgepodge (noun): a jumble of different things. "HAHJ pahj"

Think: **garage**.

If your **garage** is anything like mine, it's a **hodgepodge** of tools, old papers, junk, and who knows what else.

160

holistic (adjective): dealing with something as a whole.
"ho LIST ick"

Think: **whole list**.

Holistic medicine treats the **whole list** of body issues instead of just addressing one symptom.

homespun (adjective): simple; unpretentious.
"home SPUN"

Think: **home spun**.

Her clothes are pretty **homespun**, but then again, they actually *are* **home spun** - her mom weaves them at home on a loom.

homogeneous (adjective): having the same composition throughout. "huh MOJ in us"

Think: **homogenized** milk.

Milk is **homogenized** to mix in the cream and make a **homogeneous** liquid.

hortatory (adjective): intended to urge action.
"HORT uh tore ee"

Think: **horror story**.

The **horror story** about the spread of Ebola had a **hortatory** effect on us; we began washing our hands after touching anything.

hubris (noun): excessive pride or self-confidence.
"HYU bris"

Think: **huge breasts**.

If a girl gets implants and suddenly has **huge breasts**, she may develop **hubris** from all the male attention.

humbuggery (noun): nonsense; rubbish. "hum BUG ur ee"

Think: **bah, humbug!**

Ebenezer Scrooge said, "**bah, humbug!**" so much because he thought Christmas was **humbuggery**.

humdrum (adjective): boring. "HUM drum"

Think: **hums** and **drums**.

That was a **humdrum** band – it was just one guy who would **hum** and another guy beating a **drum**.

husbandry (noun): careful management. "HUZ bun dree"

Think: **husband**.

In the 1950s, a woman's **husband** usually practiced **husbandry** of their finances.

iconoclast (noun): someone who goes against society. "eye KON oh klast"

Think: **clashed**.

The **iconoclast** had beliefs that **clashed** with most people's views.

ideological (adjective): related to belief, sometimes at the expense of the practical. "eye dee uh LODGE ih cuhl"

Think: **idea**.

The **ideological** candidate refused to compromise on his **ideas** about what was right, winning some support but ultimately losing to his more practical opponent.

idyllic (adjective): pleasingly, naturally simple. "eye DILL ick"

Think: **ideal**.

The **idyllic** forest grove, with its sunbeams, babbling brook, and butterflies, seemed an **ideal** campsite.

163

idiosyncrasy (noun): a weird trait. "id ee oh SIN kra see"

Think: **'N SYNC-cracy**.

I might seem idiotic to suggest an **'N SYNC-cracy** where **'N SYNC** rules our nation, but it's just my **idiosyncrasy**.

ignominy (noun): deep disgrace. "IG no min-ee"

Think: **ignored many**.

Joe Paterno **ignored many** of the crimes that were being committed at Penn State; his legacy is now one of **ignominy**.

illiberal (adjective): narrow-minded. "ill LIB ur ul"

Think: **ill liberal**.

Unlike his fellow open-minded Democrats, Jack was so **illiberal** that people thought he must be a mentally **ill liberal**.

illusory (adjective): not real. "ill LOO sir ree"

Think: **illusion**.

The mirage of an oasis in the desert was an **illusion**; it was therefore **illusory**.

imbroglio (noun): complicated situation.
"im BRO glee oh"

Think: **igloo bro!**

I knew my friend was in an **imbroglio** after getting the text,
"I just woke up and I'm in an **igloo, bro!**"

imminent (adjective): about to happen. "IMM un nent"

Think: **in a moment.**

The evil-looking storm clouds told us a downpour was
imminent – it would happen **in a moment.**

immure (verb): to enclose or imprison. "imm YOUR"

Think: **in manure.**

We never should have tried to drive through this cow
pasture: our car is **immured in manure.**

immutable (noun): unchangeable. "im MUTE uh bull"

Think: **im-mutate-able.**

They poured radioactive chemicals on me to try to make
me into a mutant, but it was impossible: I'm **immutable,**
so I'm **im-mutate-able.**

impassive (adjective): unemotional. "im PASS ive"

Think: **I'm passive.**

I'm passive, and I remained **impassive** so the bully who stole my Dippin' Dots wouldn't hit me.

impeccable (adjective): flawless. "im PECK uh bull"

Think: **im-peckable.**

Due to the **impeccable** net you covered my apple tree with, the crows can't get at the fruit – it's **im-peckable.**

impecunious (adjective): poor. "imm peh Q nee us"

Think: **I'm pecking (pecuniary = related to money).**

I'm so **impecunious** that, at dinnertime, **I'm pecking** at the ground like a chicken to look for bugs to eat.

impeded (verb): blocked. "im PEED id"

Think: **stampede.**

As I walked across the fruited plain, a buffalo **stampede impeded** my progress.

imperative (adjective): very important.
"imm PEAR uh tiv"

Think: **I'm parenting!**

I'm parenting here, and I expect respect! Of course it's **imperative** that you clean your room!

imperious (adjective): dominant in a kingly way.
"im PEER ee us"

Think: **emperor.**

When we went out to dinner with the **emperor**, he was so **imperious** that he ordered all of our meals.

imperturbable (adjective): unable to be upset or excited; calm. "im purr TUR buh bull"

Think: **im (not) disturbable.**

A phone rang as I swung at the golf ball, but my **imperturbable** nature kept me from being **disturbed** and slicing the shot.

impetuous (adjective): impulsive; spontaneous.
"im PET chew iss"

Think: **impatient us**.

Impatient people like **us** make **impetuous** decisions like betting on horses with cool names without researching them first.

impetus (noun): driving force, incentive, stimulus.
"IMM pet us"

Think: **pet us**.

As dogs, our **impetus** to obey commands is that people will **pet us** as a reward.

impenetrable (adjective): unable to be penetrated (literal), unable to be understood or overcome (metaphorical).
"im PEN it truh bull"

Think: **pennant**.

In order to win the **pennant** for his team, the manager tried to make sure that his gameplan was **impenetrable** to the opposing team.

impinge (verb): to trespass on one's freedoms. "im PINJ"

Think: **I'm pinched.**

I'm pinched on the butt every time I go to that biker bar – it **impinges** on my dignity.

implacable (adjective): unable to be satisfied or pleased. "im PLAK uh bull"

Think: **im-plaque-able**

My dental hygenist was **implacable**; no matter how much I brushed and flossed, she kept telling me that my mouth was full of **plaque**.

implication (noun): a conclusion, hint, suggestion, connection or insinuation (not directly stated).
"ihm (rhymes with "him") plih KAY shun"

Think: **implying = suggesting.**

When Mike's date told him that she was tired and it was late, **implying** that was that it was time to go home, the **implication** was obvious to everyone but him. "OK, want to get some coffee then?" he asked cluelessly.

implicit (adjective): suggested but not directly expressed. "im PLISS it"

Think: **implied**.

It became **implicit** that the evening was over when my date **implied** that if she didn't leave now she would be too tired to work the next day.

imploring (verb): begging. "Im PLOR ing"

Think: **I'm poor.**

I **implore** you to lend me a few bucks since **I'm poor**.

importune (verb): to nag; to persistently insist. "im por TOON"

Think: **"I'm poor" tune**.

The homeless man at the end of my block always **importunes** us for money with his little **"I'm poor" tune**.

impregnable (adjective): unconquerable; impenetrable. "im PREG nuh bull"

Think: **impossible** to get **pregnant**.

Impregnable metal chastity belts in the Middle Ages made it **impossible** for women who wore them to get **pregnant**.

imprimatur (noun): official approval. "im prim a TURE"

Think: **imprint**.

In Game of Thrones, a king conveys his **imprimatur** with an **imprint** of his crest on a scroll's wax seal.

impromptu (adjective): without preparation.
"im PROMPT ooh"

Think: **improvise**.

If you forget your lines, I'm not going to prompt you, so just **improvise** and make some **impromptu** remarks.

impudence (noun): rudeness. "IM pew dense"

Think: **in puberty**.

Give those 12-year-olds a break. They're still **in puberty** - that's why they're so **impudent** to the substitute teacher.

impugn (verb): to attack verbally. "im PYOON"

Think: **imply ugly**.

Your insults **impugn** me; they **imply ugly** things.

inalienable (adjective): impossible to take away or give up. "In ALIEN uh bull"

Think: **in (not) alien.**

You say I'm an illegal **alien**, but I have a green card that gives me the **inalienable** right to live in the U.S.

inane (adjective): lacking meaning; silly. "in AIN (rhymes with "gain")"

Think: **insane.**

Saying you "like stuff" to describe your interests is **inane**, and it might make people think you're **insane**.

incandescent (adjective): bright; brilliant. "in can DESS sent"

Think: **candle sent.**

The **candle sent incandescent** light throughout the tomb, revealing a sleeping vampire.

incensed (adjective): extremely angry. "in SENSED"

Think: **incense.**

If you're **incensed**, smoke may be wafting off of your head as if you were a giant stick of burning **incense** (noun).

incessant (adjective): never-ending, constant. "in SESS int"

Think: **cease = to stop**

To **cease** is to stop (i.e, cease and desist), so if something is **incessant**, then it is **never-ending**. For example, when I was in college, I listened to Bob Dylan's "Basement Tapes" **incessantly**.

inchoate (adjective): incomplete; formless. "in COH it"

Think: **inches of chow**.

The pile of **chow** on the hungry man's Thanksgiving dinner place was eight **inches** high -- and created an **inchoate** blob of food.

incipient (adjective): beginning. "in SIP ee ent"

Think: **sippy cup**.

When your child's toddlerhood is **incipient** (beginning), it helps to have a good **sippy cup** to minimize the number of spills.

incisive (adjective): sharp; direct. "in SICE ive"

Think: **incision**.

Luckily, the surgeon was **incisive** - she only had seconds to make an **incision** before the patient's appendix burst.

incoherent (adjective): unclear. "in co HERE ent"

Think: **I couldn't hear it**.

Your slurred voicemail to me at 2:30 A.M. was **incoherent** - **I couldn't hear it**.

incorporate (verb): to include or take in.
"in KOR poor ate"

Think: **carp I ate**.

I don't eat much seafood, but after all that delicious **carp I ate** at the cookout, I think I should start **incorporating** more fish into my diet.

incorrigible (adjective): unable to be reformed.
"in CORE ij uh bull"

Think: **in-correctable**.

Despite his teachers' best efforts to make him sit still, the hyperactive little boy seemed **incorrigible** and **in-correctable**.

inculcate (verb): to teach by constant repetition and warning. "IN cull kate"

Think: **in cult**.

In the **cult** of Scientology, they **inculcated** Tom Cruise until he was brainwashed.

incumbent (adjective): not optional; obligatory. "in COME bent"

Think: **income bent**.

If your **income is bent** in the direction of a half-million dollars a year or more, then it is **incumbent** upon you to make sure to donate some of your money to worthy causes.

indefatigable (adjective): tireless, persistent. "in duh FAT ig uh bull"

Think: **in-defeatable**.

Because of his **indefatigable** work ethic, Michael Phelps is nearly **in-defeatable** in the pool.

indictment (noun): a criticism or accusation.
"in DAHYT (rhymes with "night") ment

Think: **dictaphone meant.**

The fact that the defendant had illegally used a **dictaphone** to record private conversations with her employer, which she later shared online, **meant** that there were grounds for an **indictment** by the court.

indigenous (adjective): native to an area. "in DIJIN us"

Think: **Indian dig in U.S.**

The archaeologist found arrowheads during her **Indian dig in the U.S.** and concluded that Native Americans were **indigenous** to the area.

indignant (adjective): offended or angered by perceived unfair treatment. "in DIG nint"

Think: **ain't diggin' it!**

When I was passed over for the promotion at work, I was **indignant**. I told my boss, "I **ain't diggin' it!**"

indomitable (adjective): unconquerable.
"in DOM it a bull"

Think: **in-dominate-able**.

Spain's national soccer team is so good that they're
indomitable or **"in-dominate-able"** - they're unable to be
dominated.

industrious (adjective): hard-working. "in DUSS tree us"

Think: maids **dusting**.

Succeeding in the cleaning industry means only hiring
industrious maids who are really good at **dusting**.

ineffable (adjective): that which cannot be described in
words. "in EFF uh bull"

Think: **in-F-able**.

There's a word beginning with "**F**" that you're not
supposed to say, so if you can't describe something, it's
ineffable - like that word is "**in-F-able**".

ineluctable (adjective): inevitable, bound to happen, certain. "in ee LUCKED a bull"

Think: **unelectable**.

It is **ineluctable** that a sex scandal on the eve of the election would render the candidate **unelectable**.

inestimable (adjective): too great to calculate. "in EST imm uh bull"

Think: **in-estimate-able**.

If something is **inestimable**, it's **in-estimate-able** – you can't estimate it.

inexorable (adjective): unstoppable. "in EX ur a bull"

Think: **in-x-out-able**.

The fighter's **inexorable** rise made it impossible to cross his name off the contender list; he was **"in-x-out-able"**.

infinitesimal (adjective): incredibly tiny. "in fin ih TESS ih mull"

Think: **infinitely small**.

Electrons are pretty much **infinitely small** - they're so **infinitesimal** that observing them changes them.

influx (noun): the arrival of many things or people. "IN flucks"

Think: **in flood**.

The **influx** of college students to Boston every September is like a **flood**.

ingenious (adjective): extremely clever. "in JEAN yiss"

Think: **genie genius**.

The **genie** granted me one wish, which I used to wish for unlimited wishes. "You're a **genius**!" he said. I know, I know.

ingenuous (adjective): completely sincere; naive. "in JEN you us"

Think: **genius without the "I" is no genius at all**.

The young actress, being an innocent **ingenue**, was too **ingenuous** to realize the director was trying to seduce her.

ingrained (adjective): deeply worked into something. "in GRAYND"

Think: **in grain**.

Pesticides sprayed on wheat will become **ingrained** into the **grain**.

179

ingratiate (verb): to make someone like you.
"in GRAY she ate"

Think: **gratitude grated**.

The new guy's excessive **gratitude grated** and seemed like an attempt to **ingratiate** himself to us.

inimical (adjective): unfriendly; hostile. "in IM ih kull"

Think: **enemy**.

Of course the other beauty contestant hid your lipstick! She's your **enemy**; it's no surprise she'll be **inimical**.

inimitable (adjective): not capable of being imitated. "in IM it a bull"

Think: **in-imitate-able**.

Michelangelo's art is **inimitable** and **in-imitate-able**; it has a magic that cannot be reproduced.

innate (adjective): existing since birth; inherent. "in NATE"

Think: **in natal**.

The ability of a spider to spin a web is not learned but **innate**; it's **in it** even in the **natal** stage before being born.

innocuous (adjective): harmless. "in NOCK you us"

Think: **innocent**.

My dog will bark at you once you come in but it's **innocent** - he's **innocuous**.

inordinate (adjective): exceeding reasonable limits. "in ORD in it"

Think: **not ordinary**.

Joey Chestnut consumed an **inordinate** number of hot dogs; it's **not ordinary** that he **ate** 62 of them.

Inscrutable (adjective): impossible to understand or interpret. "In SCREW tah bull"

Think: **in screw table**.

If I told you "in a table, there's a screw", you'd understand me, but if I said "**in a screw**, there's a **table**", I'd no doubt be **inscrutable** to you.

insinuate (verb): to hint or imply; to subtly introduce. "in SIN you ate"

Think: **in sin you ate**.

Pop culture **insinuates** that all women should be skinny, as if to say "**in sin you ate** that piece of cake".

insipid (adjective): bland; dull. "in SIP id"

Think: **in sippy**.

FYI: if your drinks are served **in sippy** cups, you're probably a baby - that's why they feed you **insipid**, mushy foods.

insolence: noun, rudeness, insensitivity. "IN suh lince"

Think: **in silence**

To punish me for my **insolence**, my kindergarten teacher forced me to sit in the corner **in silence**.

insular (adjective): narrow-minded. "IN suh lur"

Think: **insulated**.

The hermit's outlook was so **insular** because his cave **insulated** him from the rest of the world.

integrate (verb): to unite into a whole. "IN teh great"

Think: **interstate**.

The new **interstate** highway will **integrate** our town with the one in the next state since travel between the two will be easier.

interloper (noun): one who intrudes. "in tir LOPE ur"

Think: **interrupt elope.**

The **interloper interrupted** them from **eloping** when the priest said, "Speak now or forever hold your peace."

intimate (verb): to hint at. "IN tim it"

Think: **intimate** apparel.

I like my girlfriend's **intimate** (adjective) apparel because it **intimates** (verb) at the shape of her body without looking slutty.

intrepid (adjective): extremely brave. "in TREP id"

Think: **entrap it!**

Instead of running from the attacking polar bear, our **intrepid** guide handed us nets, shouting, **"entrap it!"**

intrinsic (adjective): inherent. "in TRIN zik"

Think: **twins.**

Having similar personalities is something that is comes naturally for most identical **twins**; it's **intrinsic**.

intrusive (adjective): causing disruption or annoyance by being unwelcome. "in TRUE sive"

Think: **intruder**.

We all found it to be **intrusive** when an **intruder** interrupted our Christmas morning by breaking into our house and stealing presents from under the tree.

inundated (adjective): flooded. "IN un date id"

Think: **nuns date**.

After the church allowed **nuns** to **date**, they **inundated** Match.com.

inveigh (verb): to protest or complain bitterly. "in VAY"

Think: **weigh in**.

When a person with a German accent **weighs in** on a topic which upsets him, he is **inveighing**.

inveigle (verb): to entice, lure (a person), acquire or win (a thing) through deception or flattery. "in-VAY-gull"

Think: **inveigle a bagel**.

I was able to **inveigle a bagel** by impressing the bagel store owner with my fluent Polish.

invidious (adjective): causing envy. "in VID ee us"

Think: **envious**.

I knew marrying a supermodel would make my friends **envious** – it's unfortunately an **invidious** thing to do.

inviolate (adjective): pure; intact. "in VIE oh let"

Think: **unviolated**.

The virgin tract of rainforest was **inviolate**; it had not yet been **violated** by greedy loggers.

irascible (adjective): easily angered. "ir RASS ih bull"

Think: **irritable rascal**.

My grandfather is an **irritable** old **rascal**; he's so **irascible** that he yells at every waiter we ever get.

irk (verb): to annoy. "ERRK"

Think: **jerk**.

Of course he **irks** you – he's a **jerk!**

ironic (adjective): the opposite of what one would expect. "eye RON ick"

Think: **"Hi, Ron" = ick.**

Ron's internal dialogue: "It's **ironic** that when that girl I've been crushing on finally said **"Hi, Ron,"** I just then started to lose interest in her. Sometimes I disgust myself with my self-sabotaging ways. **Ick.**"

irresolute (adjective): not firm or determined. "ear REZ oh loot"

Think: **error in resolutions.**

Looking back to January, I made an **error in making New Year's resolutions**; I'm too **irresolute** to accomplish anything besides playing video games.

jargon (noun): specialized language used by a particular group of people. "JAR gun"

Think: **Jar Jar Binks.**

Part of the problem with Star Wars' **Jar Jar Binks** was the confusing **jargon** he used when talking to Anakin Skywalker.

jejune (adjective): dull; juvenile. "jih JOON"

Think: **juvenile**.

My frat brothers' fart jokes are so **jejune** that you could almost call them **juvenile** or "**jejune**-venile".

jettison (verb): to get rid of or to reject something. "Jet ih son"

Think: **jet engine**.

After the **jet engine** failed, the pilot **jettisoned** fuel so the plane would be light enough to make it to the airport.

jingoism (noun): extreme nationalism, belligerent foreign policy. "JIN go ism"

Think: **Ringo-ism**.

The British man's **jingoism** went so far as to make him campaign for the Beatles' **Ringo** Starr to rule the free world.

jocose (adjective): given to joking. "juh KOSE"

Think: **joke coach**.

It was no surprise that the **jocose** high school student grew up to be a **joke coach**.

judicious (adjective): having good judgment.
"joo DISH us"

Think: **judgment.**

The Beatles' song "Hey **Jude**" says to be **judicious**, to use good **judgment**, and to "let her into your heart".

juggernaut (noun): something very powerful.
"JUG ur not"

Think: **juggler-knot.**

That **juggler** tied that huge **knot** by juggling six balls of yarn - it'll be a **juggernaut** to untie.

juvenescence (noun): the state of being youthful or growing young. "JOOV in ess ense"

Think: **juvenile adolescent.**

Creating **juvenescence** by partying in Vegas for his 40th birthday made the man feel like a **juvenile adolescent** again.

juxtapose (verb): to contrast. "JUCKS tuh pohz"

Think: **Huxtable**.

Cliff **Huxtable** – Bill Cosby's warm, good-natured character on *The Cosby Show* – was **juxtaposed** with his real-life persona after he was accused of rape on multiple occasions.

kindle (verb): to start; to stir up. "KIN dull"

Think: **kindling**.

You can't just light a log on fire - to **kindle** the campfire, you need some **kindling**: twigs, paper, dried grass, etc.

kindred (adjective): closely related. "KIN drid"

Think: **kind**.

I'm so **kind** to you because we're **kindred** spirits.

kismet (noun): fate. "KISS met"

Think: **kiss met**.

I knew it was **kismet** that I'd marry her because we **kissed** as soon as we **met** each other.

kowtow (verb): to kiss up to.
"COW TOWE (rhymes with "ow")

Think: **cow toes**.

If you want to **kowtow** to a farmer, **bow** and offer to give a pedicure to his **cow's toes**.

lachrymose (adjective): tearful; mournful. "lack ri MOSE"

Think: **lack Christmas**.

If you **lack Christmas** presents, I don't blame you for being **lachrymose**.

lackadaisical (adjective): without energy or spirit.
"lack a DAYS ih cull"

Think: **like a daze**.

Lackadaisical people are lazy, **like a daze** has come over them.

laconic (adjective): using few words. "luh CON ick"

Think: **lacking kick**.

His personality was **lacking kick**; he was so **laconic** that he barely even said hello to us.

lampoon (verb): to mock or satirize. "lam POON"

Think: **laugh harpoon**.

The Onion **lampooned** Kanye so skillfully that its article was like a **laugh harpoon**.

languid (adjective): lazy; lacking energy. "lan GWID"

Think: **laying squid**.

The **laying squid** was **languid** because it just lay on the bottom of the ocean all day.

largess (noun): generosity. "large ESS"

Think: **large-ness**.

Due to his wealthy parents' **largess** and the **large-ness** of their generosity, the college student lived pretty large and drove a Ferrari.

lassitude (noun): tiredness; laziness. "LASS ih tude"

Think: **lazy attitude**.

Your **lassitude** is caused by your **lazy attitude** and your belief that Lassie will come save you if you need help.

latent (adjective): existing but unseen or inactive. "LAY tent"

Think: **lay tent**.

You claim to like hiking, but your desire must be **latent** since you just **lay** in the **tent** when we camp.

laudable (adjective): worthy of praise. "LOD ih bull"

Think: **applaudable**.

Something that's **laudable** is **applaudable**.

lax (adjective): loose; not strict. "LACKS"

Think: **lacks**.

His diet plan was **lax** because he **lacks** the discipline to avoid junk food.

legerdemain (noun): sleight of hand; a display of skill. "leh jer da-MANE"

Think: **Ledger's domain**.

Heath **Ledger's domain** was the silver screen; his acting **legerdemain** captivated audiences.

lenient (adjective): forgiving, not strict. "LEEN ee ent"

Think: **loan lent**.

My bank is really **lenient** – I have terrible credit, but I asked for a **loan** and they **lent** one to me.

levity (noun): lightheartedness. "LEV ih tee"

Think: **levitate**.

The comedian's **levity** put us in such a good mood that our spirits felt as if they were **levitating**.

licentious (adjective): lacking restraint. "lie SEN shus"

Think: **license**-ish.

Flappers were thought to be **licentious**, since they acted as if they had a **license** to do whatever they wanted.

lionized (verb): treated with great interest. "LIE un ized"

Think: **lion-ized**.

The cute little meerkat was so **lionized** by the zoo's visitors that he felt like a **lion**.

listless (adjective): having little interest or energy. "LIST liss"

Think: **list-less**.

If you've never made a to-do **list**, you're **list-less** and probably **listless**.

logorrhea (noun): excessive wordiness. "log uh REE uh"

Think: **diarrhea**.

I thought a long speech would help my grade, but my teacher said my **logorrhea** was like verbal **diarrhea**.

loquacious (adjective): very talkative. "luh QUAY shus"

Think: **quack quack**.

The **loquacious** duck just wouldn't shut up: "**quack quack**, I'm a duck, **quack quack**, blah blah blah."

lovelorn (adjective): without love. "LOVE lorn"

Think: **love torn**.

After his wife died in an accident, the man felt **lovelorn**, as though he'd had his **love torn** from him.

lucid (adjective): clear; intelligible. "LOO sid"

Think: **Luz = light in Spanish**.

I'm not fully **lucid** in the morning until the sun rises and the **lug** (light) comes through the window – I can't **think clearly** while it's still dark outside because I'm still in dreamland.

lucre (noun): money; profit. "LOO kurr"

Think: **lucrative**.

When you put in the years of training necessary to secure a **lucrative** career, **lucre** is your reward.

ludicrous (adjective): ridiculous. "LOOD ih kris"

Think: **Ludacris ridiculous**.

The rapper **Ludacris** is known for his **ridiculous**, **ludicrous** lines like "I got hoes in different area codes."

lugubrious (adjective): mournful or gloomy.
"luh GOO bree us"

Think: **lug Brian**.

I became **lugubrious** when I realized I would have to **lug** the unconscious **Brian** up the stairs.

lumber (verb): to move with clumsiness. "LUM bir"

Think: **lumber** (noun).

Frankenstein would **lumber** (verb) around as if his limbs were made of **lumber** (noun).

luminary (noun): one regarded for his brilliant achievements. "LOOM in airy"

Think: **illuminate**.

It would take a **luminary** like Stephen Hawking to **illuminate** quantum physics for me.

lurid (adjective): sensational; shocking. "LURR id"

Think: **lure in**.

The strip club's **lurid** neon silhouette of a naked woman was designed to **lure in** lonely gentlemen.

macabre (adjective): gruesome; horrible. "muh COBB"

Think: **massacre**.

The **massacre** of the tourists by jungle cannibals was truly **macabre**.

macerate (verb): to weaken, break down, or make soft. "MAH sir ate"

Think: **mace**.

Spraying a mugger in the face with **mace** (tear gas) will hopefully **macerate** him.

machination (noun): a crafty scheme. "MOCK in ae shun"

Think: **machine nation**.

I don't trust C-3PO and R2D2; I bet they have **machinations** designed to create a **machine nation** in which we are slaves.

maelstrom (noun): something violently powerful; a whirlpool. "MALE strum"

Think: **mail storm**.

Spam emails flock to my inbox like a **maelstrom**; reading the **mail storm** would suck up all my time.

magisterial (adjective): having strong authority; kingly. "mah gist STEER ee ul"

Think: **Majesty**.

If people are greeting you by saying "Your **Majesty**", you're probably looking **magisterial** – wear that outfit again!

197

magnanimous (adjective): generous. "mag NAN ih muss"

Think: **magnet** for **animals**.

The "Feed the Birds" lady in *Mary Poppins* was a **magnet** for **animals** because she was so **magnanimous** to them.

magnate (noun): a powerful or influential person. "MAG nate"

Think: chick **magnet**.

You'd be a chick **magnet**, too, if you were an oil **magnate** like me.

makeshift (adjective): serving as a temporary substitute. "MAKE shift"

Think: **break shift, make shift.**

If you **break** the **shift** gears on your bike, then you might have to improvise something **makeshift** until you can get to a repair shop.

malevolent (adjective): evil. "muh LEV uh lent"

Think: **violent male.**

Malevolent criminals are usually **violent males**; most serial killers are men.

malfeasance (noun): misdeed, violation. "mal FEE zance"

Think: **mal=bad, fleas**.

The **fleas** and ants in my house commit **malfeasances** daily; I think of them as **mal (bad) fleas /** ants.

malign (verb): to speak evil of. "muh LINE"

Think: **malignant**.

The evil witch not only **maligned** her enemies but also cast spells designed to give them **malignant** tumors.

malinger (verb): to fake sickness to avoid working. "muh LIN gur"

Think: **linger**.

Those who **malinger** often **linger** in bed, pretending to have the flu.

malleable (adjective): able to be shaped. "MAL ee uh bull"

Think: **mallet-able**.

24-karat gold is so **malleable** that you can dent it with a wooden hammer - it's "**mallet-able**."

manacle (verb): to restrain. "MAN uh cuhl"

Think: **man shackle**.

These military rules manacle us just as surely as if they'd put **man shackles** on our wrists.

mandate (noun): an order or command. "MAN date"

Think: **mandatory**.

The captain's **mandate** was obviously **mandatory** – so swab the deck!

manifold (adjective): diverse; varied. "MAN ih fold"

Think: **many folds**.

The surface of the brain is **manifold** because it has **many folds**.

marginal (adjective): very limited. "MARGE in ul"

Think: **margins**.

I only had **marginal** success in deciphering the ancient manuscript because the only legible parts were the **margins**.

marshal (verb): to gather and organize. "MAR shul"

Think: fire **marshal**.

The fire **marshal's** job is to **marshal** the volunteer firemen if there's a fire alarm.

maudlin (adjective): overly sentimental. "MAWD lin"

Think: **Maude's violin**.

Maude played emotional **violin** music every time she made an entrance, so we called her **maudlin**.

mawkish (adjective): overly sentimental. "MOCK ish"

Think: **Ma's awkward kiss**.

Ma is **awkward** because she has to **kiss** us every time we leave the house - she's **mawkish**.

meager (adjective): very small; inadequate. "MEE grr"

Think: **me grr**.

These **meager** portions on this pirate ship make **me grr**.

meddle (verb): to become involved with another's affairs. "MED uhl"

Think: **middle**.

It's annoying when you **meddle** with us – you always jump into the **middle** of any quarrel we have.

meld (verb): to merge; to blend. "MELD"

Think: **melt**.

If your ice cream cup is half vanilla, half chocolate and it **melts**, the flavors will **meld**.

mellifluous (adjective): having a sweet, smooth, rich flow. "muh LIFF flu iss"

Think: **melody flow**.

Adele's **mellifluous** voice lets a **melody flow** from her lips like honey.

melodramatic (adjective): overly dramatic. "MEH low druh MATT ick"

Think: **dramatic melody**.

It's **melodramatic** to hire a violinist to follow you around and play a **dramatic melody** when you enter a room.

mendacity (noun): dishonesty. "men DAH sit ee"

Think: **mend the city**

The former mayor of Providence, Buddy Cianci, promised that he would **mend the city** and its underhanded ways, but his **mendacity** became apparent when he himself was arrested for corruption.

mendicant (noun): a beggar. "MEND ih kint"

Think: **mend? I can't!**

If you tell a **mendicant** to sew up the holes in his clothes, he'd probably say, "**mend? I can't!** They're about to fall apart."

menial (adjective): a task suitable to a servant. "MEAN ee ul"

Think: **me kneel**.

Tasks that make **me kneel**, like scrubbing the floor, are aptly called **menial**.

mephitic (adjective): foul-smelling. "meh FIT ick"

Think: **meth breath**.

I bet the devil Mephistopheles has **mephitic** breath, like that of a **meth** user.

mercenary (adjective): motivated by money.
"MURR sin erry"

Think: **merchant**.

I knew the **merchant's** compliments were insincere since he was clearly **mercenary**.

mercurial (adjective): having rapidly changing moods.
"murr CURE ee ul"

Think: **Mercury**.

Marie Curie was notorious for her **mercurial** moods, which revolved as fast as the planet **Mercury**.

meretricious (adjective): falsely attractive.
"merr (rhymes with "err") uh TRISH us"

Think: **merit tricks us**.

The sparkle of pyrite, or fool's gold, is **meretricious** because its **merit tricks us** into thinking it's a precious stone.

meterological (adj): pertaining to weather patters.
"Me tee or oh loj ih cull"

Think: **meteor logical**.

Because it's unlikely that **meteorlogical** events could have killed every living dinosaur, a **meteor** striking Earth's surface is a more **logical** explanation for their extinction.

meticulous (adjective): extremely detail-conscious.
"Meh TICK u luss"

Think: **ticks on us.**

Hiking in the woods is fun, but we need to be **meticulous** when checking our skin to make sure that there aren't any Lyme-disease-carrying **ticks on us**.

mettle (noun): strength; stamina. "MET ul"

Think: made of **metal**.

In Gladiator, Russell Crowe was so full of **mettle** he might have been made of **metal**.

miasma (noun): an unhealthy atmosphere. "mi AS muh"

Think: **my asthma**.

The smog in Los Angeles is a **miasma** that worsens **my asthma**.

microcosm (noun): a small thing representing a larger thing. "MY crow kos um"

Think: **micro-cosmos**.

The glow-in-the-dark stars on my ceiling are a **microcosm** of the universe - they're a "**micro cosmos**."

milieu (noun): setting or environment. "mill YOU"

Think: **my loo**.

I prefer to use **my loo** in my own **milieu** - other people's bathrooms are gross!

milquetoast (noun): a timid person. "MILK toast"

Think: **Milhouse / milky toast**.

Milhouse is a **milquetoast** - he's about as tough as a piece of soggy, **milky toast**, since Bart Simpson bosses him around.

mimetic (adjective): something that imitates or mimics. "mih MET ick"

Think: **mimes mimic**.

You may think **mimes** are annoying, but their **mimetic** abilities are pretty cool when they **mimic** what it would look like to be trapped in a glass box.

206

minatory (adjective): threatening. "MIN a tor ee"

Think: **minotaur**.

The **minotaur**, a creature that is half-man and half-bull, is **minatory** by nature.

minion (noun): a servant; a follower. "MIN yun"

Think: **mini-one**.

In <u>Austin Powers</u>, Mini-Me is Dr. Evil's **minion**; he is a **mini-one** of Dr. Evil.

misanthrope (noun): one who hates people. "MISS en throwpe"

Think: **mistake** to be an **anthropologist**.

It's a huge **mistake** to be an **anthropologist** and study people all day long if you're a **misanthrope**.

miscreant (noun): a person who behaves badly or in a way that breaks the law. "MISS kree int"

Think: **mistake** of **creation**.

The harsh judge believed the **miscreant** was a **mistake** of **creation**.

miserly (adjective): stingy or cheap with money.
"MY zir lee"

Think: **miserable** Scrooge.

Scrooge was **miserable** at making friends because he was too **miserly** to ever chip in for the dinner tab.

misnomer (noun): a wrong or inappropriate name.
"miss NO murr"

Think: **mis-name**.

"The Battle of Bunker Hill" is a **misnomer**: it **mis-names** the battle, which was actually fought on the nearby Breed's Hill.

mitigate (verb): to lessen or make less severe.
"MITT ih gate"

Think: **mitt gate**.

The thief wore oven **mitts** to climb the spiked **gate** of the mansion to **mitigate** the pain in his hands.

modicum (noun): a small amount. "MODD ih kum"

Think: **modest amount**.

My pet mouse is cheap to feed because a **modicum**, or **modest amount**, of food will fill up his little belly.

modish (adjective): fashionable. "MODE ish"

Think: **model-ish**.

Modish brands like Burberry and Prada are **model-ish** because only models seem to actually wear them.

monastic (adjective): strict; secluded; austere. "muh NAST ick"

Think: **monastery**.

If you're a **monk** and you live in a **monastery**, your life is probably **monastic** – no partying for you.

morass (noun): a situation that makes you stuck. "muh RASS"

Think: **molasses**.

Don't tailgate a **molasses** truck - if you run into it and it spills on you, you'll be in a **morass**.

morbid (adjective): obsessed with or overly focused on death. "MORE bid"

Think: **more bit (bite the bullet)**.

If you're **more** obsessed with **biting the bullet** than most, then you are probably a **morbid** person.

mordant (adjective): bitingly harsh, often in a funny way. "MORE dint"

Think: **Mordor**.

Those evil creatures who live in **Mordor** are especially fond of **mordant** jokes.

mores (noun): customary rules and standards. "MORES (rhymes with "snores")"

Think: **morals**.

Our society's **mores** include **morals** like helping others who are less fortunate.

moribund (adjective): dying. "MORE ih bunned"

Think: **morbid end**.

If someone is **moribund**, they're probably headed toward a **morbid end**, i.e., death.

morose: (adjective): gloomy. "muh ROWSE (rhymes with "ghost")"

Think: **no rose**.

"The Bachelor" contestant was **morose** because after the ceremony was over she still had **no rose**.

motile (adjective): having the ability to move. "MOH till"

Think: **mobile**.

Now that my one-year-old can walk, he's so **motile** that I have to be really **mobile** just to catch up to him.

motley (adjective): made up of several different parts. "MOT lee"

Think: **Motley Crue**.

The band **Motley Crue** has a **motley** history of parties, drugs, and other types of craziness.

multifaceted (adjective): having many aspects or parts. "Mull tee FASS ih ted"

Think: **multi (many) facets**.

Multifaceted diamonds sparkle because light reflects off of their **many facets**.

mundane (adjective): commonplace. "MUN dane"

Think: **Mondays**.

Asking someone if they have a "case of the **Mondays**" is such a **mundane** saying that it's not funny anymore.

munificent (adjective): generous or giving.
"moon IF uh sint"

Think: **money sent**.

The **money sent** to us by our grandparents every year makes us consider them to be **munificent**.

myopic (adjective): shortsighted. "my OP ick"

Think: **my old pic**.

Putting **my old pic** on Match.com was **myopic**; in person, people said I was older than they'd thought I'd be.

myriad (noun): a large number.
"MERE (rhymes with "here") ee id"

Think: **merry ads**.

The **myriad** of **merry ads** during the holidays tries to persuade people to spend money on presents.

nadir (noun): the lowest point. "NAY dur"

Think: **nads**.

A dude's **nads** are literally the **nadir** of his reproductive system.

212

naïveté (noun): lack of experience, wisdom or judgement. "nye eve uh TAY"

Think: **Adam and Eve**.

Some people take the creation parable of **Adam and Eve** literally, but as a scientist, I attribute that to **naïveté**.

nascent (adj): coming into existence; new. "NAH sint"

Think: **new car scent**.

I jumped into the **nascent** BMW while it was still on the assembly line and breathed in the best **new car scent** I've ever smelled.

nebulous (adjective): vague. "NEB yule us"

Think: **Nebula**.

The Horsehead **Nebula** is so many light-years away that we only have a **nebulous** idea of what it's like.

neophyte (noun): a beginner. "ne YO fight"

Think: **Neo fight**.

When **Neo** has his first **fight** with an agent in <u>The Matrix</u>, he is a **neophyte** and gets his ass kicked.

nepotism (noun): unfairly hiring family. "NEP oh TIS um"

Think: **nephew favoritism**.

They said I practiced **nephew favoritism** and accused me of **nepotism** when I promoted my 22-year-old nephew to vice president of the company.

nettle (verb): to irritate. "NET ul"

Think: **needle**.

Poking someone with a **needle** is a quick way to **nettle** him.

newfangled (adj): new, often needlessly so.
"nu FANG ulled"

Think: **new tangled**.

This **newfangled** yo-yo is so **new** to me that it's **tangled** around my entire body.

noisome (adjective): stinky. "NOICE um"

Think: **nose poison**.

The boys' locker room is **noisome**; going in there is like taking **nose poison**.

214

non sequitur (n): something unrelated.
"non SECK quit ur"

Think: **not sequence.**

Bringing up koala bears after my girlfriend asked me about our relationship was a **non sequitur**; it was **not** in the right **sequence.**

nonchalant (adjective): acting casual or disinterested.
"non shuh LAUNT (rhymes with "flaunt")"

Think: **non-challenge**

I'm **nonchalant** when I ask out a girl; it's really a **non-challenge** for me since I've got so much game.

nondescript (adjective): plain. "non duh SCRIPPED"

Think: **no description.**

The little desert island was so **nondescript** that it had **no description** in our guidebook.

nonpareil (adjective): having no equal. "non pear ELL"

Think: **no parallel.**

The master parachutist had **nonpareil** skill; he truly had **no parallel** in the parachuting field.

nonplussed (adj): bewildered or confused.
"non PLUSSED"

Think: **no plus**.

The calculator you loaned me made me **nonplussed** during the test because it had **no plus** button.

nontrivial (adjective): not unimportant. "non TRIV ee ul"

Think: **trivia**.

Most of the questions they ask during **trivia** night at the bar are rather **trivial** if you ask me...but my pop-culture-loving roommate finds them **nontrivial**.

normative (adjective): prescribing a standard or model. "NORM a tive"

Think: **normal.**

Are you **normal**? If you said, "yes", then are you buying into someone else's **normative** rules of behavior?

nostalgia (noun): a bittersweet longing for the past. "nuh STAL guh"

Think: **nose tampon.**

My **nostalgia** for my glory days got so bad that I had to use a **nose tampon** for my constant sniffles.

nostrum (noun): a questionable medicine or remedy. "NAH strum"

Think: **nostril rum**.

The Simpsons' Dr. Nick's **nostrum** was **nostril rum** - rum meant to be snorted to clear the sinuses.

notorious (adjective): famous for being bad. "no TORY us"

Think: **Notorious B.I.G.**

The **Notorious B.I.G.** got away with calling himself **notorious** since he sold crack as a youth.

novel (adjective): strikingly new. "NAW vul"

Think: **novice**.

When I was an internet **novice**, the idea of email was **novel** to me.

novitiate (noun): a beginner. "no VISHY it"

Think: **novice initiate**.

The **novitiate** is a **novice** frat brother, so they'll **initiate** him by making him run around campus wearing a thong.

noxious (adjective): harmful. "NOCK shus"

Think: **toxic**.

Burning plastic releases **noxious** fumes that are **toxic** to living things.

nuance (noun): a subtle or slight distinction.
"NEW aunts (rhymes with "flaunts")"

Think: **new ants**.

Forgive me for not picking up on the **nuance** of today's experiment - I couldn't tell it had **new ants** compared to yesterday's - ants all look the same to me.

nugatory (adjective): unimportant. "NOOG a-tory"

Think: negative **nuggets**.

Eating chicken **nuggets** is **nugatory** for good health; their health benefits could be said to be negative.

obdurate (adjective): hardened; stubbornly persistent. "ob DUR it "

Think: **obstacle durable**.

That 10-ton boulder you blocked my front door with is an **obstacle** that's **durable** - I tried to push it, but it's **obdurate**.

218

obeisance (noun): a gesture to show respect. "oh BEY since"

Think: **obey stance**.

When the natives bowed to the conqueror in **obeisance**, it was like an "**obey stance**".

obfuscated (verb): made unclear. "awb fusk KATED"

Think: **obstacles confused**.

The professor barely spoke English: the **obstacles** his speech created **confused** us and **obfuscated** his message.

objectionable (adjective): undesirable; offensive. "Obb JECT shin a bull"

Think: **Objection!**

Objection, your honor! The plantiff's attorney just mooned me - behavior which is clearly **objectionable**.

objective (adjective): not influenced by personal perspective. "ob JECT ive"

Think: **object**.

It's easy to have an **objective** opinion about an **object** like a rock – there's not much debate about what a rock is.

objurgation (noun): a harsh reprimand or criticism.
"ob jur GAY shun"

Think: failed **obligation.**

When I got married I took on the **obligation** to be faithful, so I wasn't surprised when my wife gave me a severe **objurgation** after I cheated on her.

obloquy (noun): harshly critical statements; being discredited. "OB la quee"

Think: **lob queries**.

The prosecutor kept **lobbing queries** at the witness in an attempt to discredit him through **obloquy**.

obsequious (adj): too eager to help or obey.
"ob SEE quee us"

Think: **obscene kiss ass**.

I can't believe that **obsequious** guy got the promotion – he's just an **obscene kiss ass**.

obstinate (adjective): stubborn. "OB stin-nit"

Think: **obstacle in it**.

The **obstinate** horse behaved as though there was an **obstacle** to movement **in it**.

obstreperous (adjective): stubbornly resistant to control; noisy. "ob STREP er-us"

Think: **strep**.

The bacteria that cause **strep** throat are so **obstreperous** that many people take antibiotics for the condition.

obtrusive (adjective): noticeable in an unwelcome way. "obb TRUE sive"

Think: O.B.T.

You're right – I'm not really listening to you. But it's because there's an **O.B.T.** (**O**range **B**aboon **T**arantula) under the table that keeps trying to crawl up my leg in an **obtrusive** way.

occluded (adjective): closed up; blocked. "awk LEWDED"

Think: **Octomom cluttered**.

Octomom cluttered the hospital's nursery with her eight babies and **occluded** it so no other infants were admitted.

odious (adj): arousing or deserving hatred. "OH dee-us"

Think: **odorous** onions.

Only eating onions is **odious** because they make one's breath so **odorous**.

officious (adjective): bossy. "oh FISH us"

Think: **vicious official**.

The **official** was **vicious** enough to measure every fish we caught with a ruler to make sure it was legal.

offset (verb): to have the opposite effect; to balance. "off SET"

Think: **offs it**.

Seeing a beautiful woman light up a cigarette **offsets** my interest in her; it effectively **offs it** since smoking is gross.

ogle (verb): to stare at in a way that shows excessive desire. "OH gull"

Think: **Google.**

Half of my **Google** searches are for swimsuit models since I like to **ogle** them.

omission (noun): something not done or missed. "oh MISSION"

Think: **miss**

My Oscar speech was marred by my **omission** of my agent; I can't believe I **missed** thanking him.

omniscient (adjective): all-knowing. "om NISH ent"

Think: **owns his science**.

I'm not surprised to hear that Jesus got an A in AP Chem; he **owns his science** classes because he's **omniscient**.

onus (noun): burden; obligation. "OWN us"

Think: **on us**.

Since we broke the vase, the **onus** is **on us** to pay for it.

opaque (adjective): something that is cloudy, blurry, or difficult to understand. "oh PAKE"

Think: an **opaque lake**.

If you don't want to get sick, then I don't recommend swimming in an **opaque lake**.

openhanded (adjective): generous. "OH pen HAN ded"

Think: **open** your **hand**.

To be **openhanded**, **open** your **hand** and share what you have with others instead of keeping it clenched in your fist.

opine (verb): to hold or state as an opinion. "OH pine"

Think: **opinion**.

If you **opine** about the election on Facebook, everyone gets to hear your **opinion** whether they like it or not.

opportune (adjective): well-timed. "ah por TUNE"

Think: **opportunity**.

It's **opportune** that I got picked for this singing **opportunity** because a genie just granted my wish to sing perfectly.

opprobrium (noun): public disgrace. "oh PRO bree-um"

Think: **Oprah opposes**.

Sometimes, **Oprah** brings people she **opposes** on her show to cause them **opprobrium** - it's like "**Oprah-brium**".

opulent (adj): very expensive and comfortable. "OPP you lent"

Think: **opal**

I just ordered one thousand **opals** from the jeweler – I want my new office to be **opulent**.

ornate (adjective): elaborately or excessively decorated. "or NATE"

Think: **ornaments**.

Ornaments covered every inch of the Christmas tree due to the decorator's **ornate** style.

orthodox (adj): conventional; traditional. "orth oh DOCKS"

Think: **orthodontist**.

Look for an **orthodox orthodontist**; you don't want someone getting creative with your teeth.

oscillate (verb): to vary; to go back and forth. "AW sill ate"

Think: **Ozzy**.

On MTV's *The Osbornes*, **Ozzy oscillates** between sanity and insanity.

ossified (verb): became hard or inflexible. "AW sih fied"

Think: **fossil-fied**.

The Velociraptor's bones could bend slightly, but after death, they **ossified** and turned into **fossils**.

ostentatious (adjective): showy; pretentious; boastful. "aw sten TAY shus"

Think: **ostrich stunt**.

That **ostrich stunt** - when you showed up at the prom riding one like a horse - was **ostentatious**.

ostracized (verb): excluded. "AW struh-sized"

Think: **ostrich-sized**.

That poor kid is **ostrich-sized** – he'll be **ostracized** as soon as he starts high school.

otiose (adjective): useless; lazy. "OH she ose"

Think: **tortoise** fetch.

Playing fetch with this **tortoise** is **otiose**.

outmoded (adjective): out of date. "out MO ded"

Think: **Apple Pie a la mode**.

Apple pie a la mode (with vanilla ice cream on top) is a tasty but **out-of-date** dessert: I can see someone ordering it at a 1950s diner.

outstrip (verb): to outrun or to exceed. "out STRIP"

Think: **out-strip**.

To be fair, that **stripper** gets more tips than you because her pole-dancing skills **outstrip** yours.

overshadow (verb): to be more important than. "oh ver SHAH dow"

Think: **shadow over**.

Hanging out with LeBron is rough; not only do his skills **overshadow** mine on the court, but he's so tall that even his **shadow** towers **over** me.

overweening (adjective): arrogant. "oh ver WEEN ing"

Think: **weenie**.

The young actor's demands were so **overweening** that the movie crew started calling him a **weenie** behind his back.

pacific (adjective): soothing. "pa SIF ick"

Think: **pacifier**.

The infant's **pacifier** had a **pacific** effect, and she was soon asleep.

painstaking (adjective): very careful. "PAINS taking"

Think: **taking pains**.

Taking pains to not infect the patient means being **painstaking** when you wash your hands before surgery.

palatable (adjective): tasty. "PAL it ah-bull"

Think: **pal at table**.

Having my **pal at** the **table** for dinner seems to make the food more **palatable** since I'm in a good mood.

palatial (adjective): magnificent. "puh LAY shull"

Think: **palace**.

The **palatial** resort, with luxurious amenities and gourmet food, was like a **palace**.

palimpsest (noun): something with multiple layers, changes, or meanings. "PA lim sest"

Think: **pa's lamp set**.

Pa's lamp set was more than just a bunch of lamps: it was also a piece of modern art with **multiple shades of meaning**.

pall (noun): something that covers; a feeling of gloom. "Paul"

Think: **pallbearers**.

Looking back, it was a mistake to invite the **pallbearers** to our party. As soon as they entered, carrying that coffin, a **pall** settled over the room.

palliate (verb): to reduce the severity of. "PAL ee ate"

Think: **pill I ate**.

The prescription **pill I ate** should **palliate** my depression.

pallid (adjective): lacking color. "PAL id"

Think: **pale**.

After playing video games in his mother's basement all winter, Al was so **pale** his friends described him as **pallid**.

panacea (noun): a cure-all. "pan uh SEE uh"

Think: **pan of** Vitamin **C**.

The hippie advised me that eating a **pan of** vitamin **C** is a **panacea** for illness.

pander: (verb): to appeal to someone's desire for selfish reasons. "PAN dur"

Think: **panda** logo.

The American company that used a **panda** as its logo was accused of **pandering** to the Chinese market.

pangs (noun): sharp feelings of pain. "Pangs"

Think: **pains**.

I read *The Hunger Games* for six hours, but then had to stop because of the **pains** from my own hunger **pangs**.

panned (verb): sharply criticized. "Panned"

Think: **frying pan**.

My first movie got **panned** so badly by critics that they might as well have hit me with a **frying pan**.

paradigm (noun): an example used as a pattern or model. "par uh DIME"

Think: **pair of dimes**.

Those two girls are a **pair of dimes** since they're both 10s – they're **paradigms** for how to look hot.

paragon (noun): a model of excellence. "PAR uh GONE"

Think: **Aragorn**.

If you're looking for a **paragon** in <u>The Lord of the Rings</u>, choose **Aragorn**: he became the king.

pariah (noun): an outcast. "purr I uh"

Think: **Mariah's** anthem.

Mariah Carey became a **pariah** after butchering the national anthem in front of 80,000 fans.

parley (verb): to talk. "PAR lee"

Think: **parsley**.

If you're going to **parley** with someone you like, eat some **parsley** - it's good for your breath.

parochial (adjective): narrow-minded. "purr RO key-ul"

Think: **parish yokel**.

Our church is led by a **parish yokel** who is so **parochial** that he believes women should be barefoot and pregnant.

parody (noun): a mocking or satirical imitation.
"par uh DEE"

Think: **parrot-y**.

Pro tip: a good way to make fun of someone is to repeat what he just said in a squawky **parrot-y** voice, to **parody** him.

paroxysm: (noun): an attack, spasm, or outburst.
"par ROX cism"

Think: **paradox spasm**.

If you drink ocean water, you'll have a **paroxysm** – it's a **paradox** that it's water but it causes **spasms** if you swallow it.

parsimonious (adjective): stingy. "par si MOAN nee us"

Think: **parsley money**.

My dad was so **parsimonious** he'd give us **parsley money** instead of lunch money.

partiality (noun): an (often unfair) liking or bias toward something. "Par she AL it ee"

Think: **Porsche.**

If anyone is having trouble deciding what to get me for my birthday this year, I have a **partiality** toward **Porsches**.

partisan (adjective): biased toward one side. "PART ih-sun"

Think: **Party's son.**

The chairman of the Democratic **Party's son** was understandably **partisan** about politics.

pastiche (noun): an imitation; something made of many things. "pass TICHE"

Think: **paste each.**

If you copy Wikipedia and **paste each** entry into your paper, it will be a **pastiche**.

pathos (noun): a quality that evokes feelings of sadness or pity. "PATH owes

Think: **sympathy ohhhs.**

Your painting of a starving puppy has so much **pathos** that it always gets **sympathy** "**ohhhs**" from viewers.

233

patois (noun): the speech/slang used by a certain group. "pa TWAH"

Think: **patio speech**.

Patio speech during barbecues is more likely to contain **patois** than speech in the office.

paucity (noun): lack of. "PAW city"

Think: **poor city**.

In the **poor city**, there was a **paucity** of resources.

pedantic (adjective): teacherly; overly fussy. "peh DAN tick"

Think: **Dan ticked me off**.

Dan ticked me off when he was being overly **pedantic**, **explaining** every facet of his computer to me as if I were a child.

pedestrian (adjective): dull; ordinary. "peh DEST ree en"

Think: **pedestrian** (noun).

You're **pedestrian** (adjective) because you're a **pedestrian** (noun) – cool kids drive to school.

peevish (adjective): irritable; whiny; bratty. "PEE vish"

Think: **pet peeve.**

In the *Harry Potter* books, Peeves is a **peevish** ghost in Hogwarts whose **pet peeve** is happy students - so he tattletales on them.

penchant (noun): a liking for something. "PEN shent"

Think: **pendant enchant.**

If a girl wears a low hanging **pendant** to **enchant** the boys, they'll soon have a **penchant** for her.

pendulous (adjective): hanging loosely; sagging. "PEN dew luss"

Think: **pendulum.**

As the naked old lady danced, her **pendulous** breasts swung back and forth like the **pendulums** of grandfather clocks.

penitent (adjective): being sorry for one's actions. "PEN ih tent"

Think: **repent!**

The beggar's sign read, "**repent!** Do penance for your sins! Only the **penitent** will see God!"

penurious (adjective): stingy. "peh NUR y us"

Think: **penny furious**.

The **penny** tip made the waiter **furious**; the customer must have been **penurious**.

penury (noun): severe poverty. "PEN ur y"

Think: **penalty**.

The court's **penalty** was so large that the defendant suffered from **penury** to the point of only owning one penny.

peons (noun): lower-class workers used by someone of a superior class. "PEE ins"

Think: **pee-ons**.

The nobleman so little respected his **peons** that he would **pee on** them.

peregrinate (verb): to journey or travel from place to place. "PERR (rhymes with "err") ih grin ate"

Think: **peregrin** falcon.

The fastest member of the animal kingdom is the **peregrin** falcon; it exceeds 200 m.p.h. while diving and can **peregrinate** speedily.

peremptory (adjective): bossy, prone to cutting others off.
"puh REMP tuh ree"

Think: **pre-empted**.

The Emperor **pre-empted** Luke's replies so much that even Darth Vader called him **peremptory**.

perennial (adjective): constant; persistent; recurring.
"purr ANY ul"

Think: **per annual**.

Per the **annual** tradition, it's time to start the **perennial** search for the next American Idol.

perfidy (noun): treachery; treason. "PURR-FIH-dee"

Think: **perforated fidelity**.

When I realized my friend spread rumors about me, I felt like he had **perforated fidelity** because of his **perfidy**.

perfunctory (adj): showing little interest.
"purr FUNKED ur y"

Think: **per function** problem.

I know I won't get them right, so I only spend a **perfunctory** amount of time **per function** problem.

peripatetic (adjective): wandering; traveling; constantly moving from place to place. "Peh ruh puh TET ick"

Think: **pitter-patter**.

The mouse in my house is **peripatetic** since I'm constantly hearing the **pitter-patter** of his little feet in the walls.

peripheral (adjective): off to the side, external, related, tangential. "purr RIFF ur-ull"

Think: **Perry Farrell**.

Perry Farrell, the eccentric founder of Lollapalooza, has never made into the musical mainstream; he seems to prefer the **peripheral** genres.

permeated (verb): spread through; penetrated. "PERM y ated"

Think: **perm he ate**.

The **perm he ate** will **permeate** his stomach lining and prove it's stupid to eat human hair.

permutation (noun): a transformation or rearrangement. "PERM you TAY shun"

Think: **mutation**.

A radioactive spider bite caused a **permutation** of Peter Parker's genes and caused his **mutation** into Spiderman.

pernicious (adjective): destructive; deadly. "per NISH iss (rhymes with "kiss")"

Think: **piranhas vicious**.

Piranhas are **vicious**; lingering in waters they inhabit can be **pernicious**.

perquisites (noun): privileges or bonuses. "PER quiz its"

Think: **perks**.

Hey suckahs - now that I'm CEO, I enjoy **perquisites** like a company helicopter and a gold wastebasket - **perks** you'll never have.

personified (verb): to be the perfect example of something; to represent a thing as a person.
"purr SAHN if eyed"

Think: **person.**

Look up "greatness" in the dictionary and the **person** in the picture is me; I'm greatness **personified**.

perspicacious (adjective): sharp; clever.
"purse puh-KAY shiss (rhymes with "kiss")"

Think: **perspective** for the **aces.**

A **perspicacious** poker player uses her clear **perspective** to know who has the **aces.**

pertinacious (adjective): stubbornly persistent.
"purr tin aey shuss"

Think: **persistent** and **tenacious.**

My **pertinacious** defender was both **persistent** and **tenacious**; I had no open shots.

perturb (verb): to disturb greatly. "purr TURB"

Think: **disturbed** by **turds.**

The **turds** your dog leaves on my beautiful lawn not only **disturb** me - they **perturb** me.

pervasive (adjective): widespread, prevalent, omnipresent. "purr VAY sive (rhymes with "give")"

Think: **perv invasive**.

That **perv** is so **invasive** – his inappropriate touching is **pervasive** and goes way over the line.

perverse (adjective): bad; wrong; corrupt. "purr VERSE"

Think: **perverts**.

Perverts like Peeping Toms are **perverse**; they should be locked up.

petulant (adjective): rude; irritable. "PETCH you lent"

Think: **petty aunt**.

My **petty aunt** is always whining about something or holding a grudge; she's **petulant**.

philander (verb): to have casual or unfaithful sex. "fi LAND urr"

Think: **Zoolander**.

When you're ridiculously good-looking like **Zoolander**, it's easy to **philander**.

phlegmatic (adjective): sluggish; unresponsive.
"fleg MATIC"

Think: **phlegm**.

When I had the flu, I had so much **phlegm** clogging my respiratory system that I was completely **phlegmatic**.

physiological (adjective): related to the body.
"fizz y yo LOG ih cull"

Think: **physical**.

I knew I wasn't just imagining I was ill because my **physiological** symptom, a fever of 103, was **physical**.

picaresque (adjective): about someone's adventures.
"pick a RESK"

Think: **Pixar-esque**.

Your novel is like Wall-E because of your hero's journey; it's both **picaresque** and **Pixar-esque**.

picayune (adjective): unimportant; small-minded.
"pick a YUNE"

Think: **picky one**.

The **picayune** bridezilla was quite the **picky one**, worrying about every single detail of her wedding.

picturesque (adjective): lovely. "pick sure ESK"

Think: **pictures**.

The Grand Canyon at sunrise is so **picturesque** that you can't help but take **pictures**.

piebald (adjective): many-colored; varied. "PIE bulled"

Think: **pies**.

The horse's coat was **piebald**, pebbled with blotches of so many colors that it looked like **pies** were thrown at it.

pilfer (verb): to steal. "PILL fur"

Think: **pill for**.

Here's an idea: we break into the pharmacy and **pilfer pills for** resale to drug addicts.

pillory (verb): to publicly and harshly criticize. "PILL ur y"

Think: **Hillary**.

Republicans love to **pillory Hillary** Clinton.

pinnacle (noun): the highest point of something. "PIN a cull"

Think: **Pinocchio.**

Pinocchio is the story of Geppetto, a woodworker, whose **pinnacle** of achievement is carving a wooden boy (**Pinocchio**) who can move and talk.

pioneering (adj): earliest; original. "PIE-oh NEAR-ing"

Think: **pioneer.**

Lewis and Clark, the **pioneers** that led the first American expedition to the Pacific coast, were **pioneering** explorers.

piquant (adjective): pleasantly spicy or tangy. "PEEK ent"

Think: **pickled ant.**

I never thought I'd like eating **pickled ant**, but it's surprisingly **piquant**.

pitfall (noun): drawback. "PIT fall"

Think: **pit fall.**

We prepared for lots of dangers before our jungle trek, but funnily enough, our biggest **pitfall** was an actual **pit fall**.

244

pith (noun): the essential or central part.
"PITH (rhymes with "with")"

Think: **pit**.

If you're a peach tree, the **pith** of your fruit is the **pit**, since that's how you'll reproduce.

pittance (noun): a very small amount. "PIT ints"

Think: **pit ants**.

Pit ants are known for eating even the **pittance** of fruit that clings to discarded peach pits.

pivotal (adjective): important, key. "PIV it ul"

Think: **pivot foot**

In basketball, knowing how to effectively use your **pivot foot** is **pivotal** to your success in the low post. Just ask Hakeem "The Dream" Olajuwon or Kevin McHale.

placate (verb): to pacify or satisfy an angry or difficult person. "PLAY kate"

Think: **play Kate.**

In order to **placate** my attention-loving sister, I told her that she could **play Kate** Winslet's lead characer in our theater's adaptation of *Titanic*.

245

plaintive (adjective): melancholy.
"PLANE tive (rhymes with "give")"

Think: **complaint**.

When I hear the **plaintive** cry of a seagull, it always sounds like a **complaint** about the bird's woes or travails.

platitude (noun): an overused expression.
"PLAT (rhymes with "bat") ih tude"

Think: **blah attitude**.

Dude, she's giving you that **blah attitude** cause your pickup line was a **platitude**.

platonic (adjective): not related to romance or sex.
"Pluh TAWN ick"

Think: **Plato** date.

If you only talk to your date about the philosopher **Plato**, you'll end up as her **platonic** friend.

plaudits (noun): approval. "PLAUD its"

Think: **applaud it**.

If you want to give **plaudits** to his work, **applaud it**.

plausible (adjective): apparently true. "PLAWS ih bull"

Think: **applause-able**.

When the magician sawed the lady in half, it looked so **plausible** that it was **applause-able**.

plebeian (adjective): common; low-class. "PLEE be in"

Think: **fleas be in**.

I don't stay in **plebeian** motels 'cause **fleas be in** 'em.

plenipotentiary (adjective): fully empowered.
"Plen a po TENT cha ry"

Think: **plenty** of **potency**.

If Romney wins the election, he will be **plenipotentiary**; being president will give him **plenty** of **potency**.

pluck (noun): courage; spirit. "PLUK"

Think: **pluck** a feather.

You showed **pluck** by attempting to **pluck** a feather from a live ostrich; too bad it decided to peck you in the eye.

plutocracy (noun): government controlled by the wealthy. "plue TOCK ra see"

Think: **Pluto** vacation home.

Hearing about the senator's vacation home on **Pluto** made me realize we're in a **plutocracy**.

polarize (verb): to separate into two conflicting or opposite positions. "PO la rise"

Think: Earth's **poles**.

Democrats and Republicans are so **polarized** that I'm surprised they don't stay at the North and South **Poles** to keep as far apart as they can.

polemic (noun): a harsh attack against a principle. "po LEM ick"

Think: **politician** at a **mic**.

Put a **politician** at a **mic**, and you'll soon hear **polemic** as he attacks his opponent's policies.

politesse (noun): politeness. "paw lit ESS"

Think: **politeness**.

French maids are trained to show **politeness** at all times; their **politesse** is without equal.

politic (adjective): shrewd; wise. "PAW lit ick"

Think: **politician**.

After reading *The Prince* by Machiavelli, the **politician** became much more **politic** and cleverly defeated his opponent.

pomp (noun): ceremony and showy display. "PAWMP"

Think: **pump**.

The bodybuilder was all about **pomp**; before he went to the beach, he worked out to get a **pump** to show off his muscles.

ponderous (adjective): heavy; dull. "PON dur us"

Think: **ponder**.

If a subject in school makes you **ponder** it for long periods of time, it could just be that it's **ponderous** and is either heavy, or dull, or both.

portentous (adjective): foreshadowing something bad; trying to seem important. "Poor TENT shis"

Think: **important tent**.

It's **important** that we set up our **tent**; those thunderclouds look **portentous**.

poseur (noun): one who pretends to be something he is not. "po ZERR (rhymes with "err")"

Think: **poser.**

The **poseur** pretended to be interested in literature to impress girls, but he was exposed as a **poser** who didn't even know who Shakespeare was.

posit (verb): to assume to be true; to suggest. "PAUSE it"

Think: **positive.**

Positive about her findings, the scientist finally agreed to **posit** the existence of extraterrestrial life in a journal article.

posthumous (adjective): after death.
"PAWST (rhymes with "lost") hyu miss"

Think: **post-human.**

It's a small comfort to be **posthumously** awarded a medal – you're **post-human** at that point, i.e., dead.

pragmatic (adjective): practical. "prag MATICK"

Think: **practical automatic.**

To be **practical**, buy an **automatic** car instead of a stick shift - it's more **pragmatic** for city driving.

prattle (noun): meaningless talk. "PRAT ul"

Think: baby **rattle**.

Her **prattle** about reality TV was as exciting as listening to a baby shake its **rattle**.

precarious (adjective): dangerously unstable. "pruh CARE y us"

Think: **preach carefulness**.

Preach carefulness to people who are standing on **precarious** rock ledges.

precocious (adjective): very talented at a young age. "pruh CO shus"

Think: **pre-coaching**.

Sadie was **precocious** at piano **pre-coaching**; she taught herself to play Mozart at the age of two.

precursor (noun): something that came before another thing. "PRE kur sir"

Think: **pre-cursor**.

When you're typing, the word you just typed is literally **pre-cursor**; it's before the cursor and is thus a **precursor** to it.

predilection (noun): a preference. "pre dih LECT shun"

Think: **predicted direction**.

Google **predicted** the **direction** of my search when I typed "how to find" by showing "how to find love", because it knows people have a **predilection** to seek romance.

premonition (noun): hunch, intuition. "preh mo NISH UN"

Think: **pre-mention**.

I knew you were going to say that! I had a **premonition pre** (before) you **mentioned it**.

prescient (adjective): seeing the future; well-planned and thought out. "PRESS y ent"

Think: knowing about **present** you **sent**.

Since I'm **prescient**, I already know what's in the **present** you **sent** me.

pretext (noun): a fake excuse. "PRE text"

Think: **pee text**.

She pretends to have to **pee** and leaves on the **pretext** of using the restroom so she can **text** without getting caught.

prevarication (noun): a lie. "pruh VARE uh kay shun"

Think: **pre-verification.**

Pre-verification, your story about getting chased by a bear was believable, but your friend just confirmed the animal was a squirrel, exposing your **prevarication.**

primed (adjective): ready. "PRYMED"

Think: **primed for prime time.**

When a television news anchor has paid her dues, you might say that she's **primed for prime time.**

primordial (adjective): original; existing since the beginning. "Pry MORDY ul"

Think: **primary order.**

The Big Bang is **primordial** because it has the **primary** position in the **order** of events.

pristine (adjective): pure. "prih STEEN"

Think: **Listerine.**

Listerine mouthwash tastes bad but it kills bacteria and makes your mouth **pristine.**

proclivity (noun): a tendency, inclination, or predisposition toward a particular activity. "pro CLIVE ih tee"

Think: **pro-cliff tee**

I'm guessing that the guy with the **pro-mountain climbing t-shirt** has a **proclivity** for extreme sports, since he climbs **cliffs**.

prodigal (adj): wasteful. "PROD ih gull"

Think: **Prada gal.**

The **Prada gal** was **prodigal:** she spent all her money on designer clothes.

prodigious (adjective): impressively large; extraordinary. "prah DIJ us"

Think: **prodigy**.

The child **prodigy** could multiply **prodigious** numbers in his head.

profane (adjective): sacrilegious; vulgar; improper. "proh FAIN"

Think: **profanity**.

Using **profanity** in church is obviously **profane**.

profligacy (noun): reckless wastefulness.
"prah FLIG a-see"

Think: **profits fling**.

If your **profits fling** out the window, you're probably following a course of **profligacy**.

profound (adjective): deep. "pro FOUND"

Think: **professor found**.

My **professor found** the cure for cancer because his decades of study gave him a **profound** understanding of the disease.

profuse (adjective): plentiful; abundant. "pro FYOOS"

Think: **professors use**.

Professors use books with a **profuse** amount of information to make reading assignments take forever.

progenitors (noun): direct ancestors.
"pro JEN ih ters (rhymes with "hers")"

Think: **produced** from **genitals**.

You were **produced** from the **genitals** of your **progenitors**.

prognosticate (verb): to predict. "Prog NAWS tih-kate"

Think: **professional knows**.

Punxsutawney Phil, the groundhog who **prognosticates** whether winter will last for six more weeks, is obviously a **professional** that **knows** the future.

proliferate (verb): to grow or multiply quickly.
"pro LIFF ur ate"

Think: **pro-life-rate**.

The **pro-life-rate** of births is higher than the pro-choice rate; pro-life people **proliferate** because they don't get abortions.

prolific (adjective): abundantly productive. "pro LIFF ick"

Think: **pro-life-ic**.

That state is anti-abortion, and they're **prolific** baby-makers because of their **pro-life-ic** stance on the subject.

prolix (adjective): too long / wordy. "PRO licks"

Think: **prolific**.

After writing dozens of 1000+ page books, the **prolific** author was often criticized for his **prolix** writing style.

prominent (adjective): well-known; standing out. "PRAH min int"

Think: **Prom King.**

The **Prom King** is usually not the shy boy that no one knows; he's often a **prominent**, popular kid.

promulgate (verb): to make known. "PROM ul gate"

Think: **promote mullet.**

The hillbilly hairstylist would often **promote mullets** by **promulgating** about them to new clients.

pronounced (adjective): noticeable. "pruh NOUNCED"

Think: **pronounced (verb).**

My British friend enunciates very loudly and distinctly; his **pronunciation** is quite **pronounced**.

propagate (verb): breed, grow, promote, publicize. "PROP a gate"

Think: **proper gait.**

The first step to **propagating** your DNA is to cultivate the **proper gait**: in other words, you have to learn how to look good while walking.

propensity (noun): a tendency, inclination, or predisposition toward a particular activity. "pro PEN si-tee"

Think: **vaporizer pen.**

The newest generation of smokers has a **propensity** to use **vaporizer pens** since they're purported to be safer than traditional cigarettes, but experts aren't sure whether they actually are less harmful.

prophetic (adjective): that which foretells the future. "prah FET ick"

Think: **prophet.**

In the bible, Jesus is considered to be a **prophet** because many of his **prophetic** claims actually happened - like predicting that Peter would deny him three times.

propitious (adjective): favorable; promising. "pro PISH us"

Think: **prop it up.**

In "A Charlie Brown Christmas", Linus thought the little tree was **propitious**, so he decided to **prop it up**.

propriety (noun): the quality of being proper or appropriate. "pro PRY it y"

Think: **proper**.

For the sake of **propriety**, use **proper** manners and eat your salad with the salad fork, not the dinner fork.

prosaic (adjective): dull or boring. "pro SAY ick"

Think: **pros say ick**.

I was going to watch the new Adam Sandler movie, but the movie critic **pros say**, "**ick** - the film is **prosaic**".

protean (adjective): varied; versatile. "PRO tee-in"

Think: **proteins**.

Since they can be formed from a vast number of combinations of 500 different amino acids, **proteins** are **protean**.

providential (adjective): favorable, fortunate, timely. "prah vih DEN shull"

Think: **Pro-V Dental**.

The friendly representative from **Pro-V Dental** insurance company helped me create a policy just one week before I accidentally chipped my tooth. It was quite **providential**. (providence = fate)

provincial (adjective): narrow-minded. "prah VIN shull"

Think: **province**.

If you never leave your Canadian **province**, your worldview will probably be somewhat **provincial**.

prowess (noun): exceptional bravery and/or skill. "PROW (rhymes with "how") ess"

Think: **prowl lioness**.

While on the **prowl**, the **lioness** displayed her **prowess** by bringing down a woolly mammoth.

proximity (noun): closeness. "prock SIM ih tee"

Think: **approximately**.

Approximately means "close to"; **proximity** means closeness.

prudent (adjective): wise. "PROO dent"

Think: **prude student**.

In high school, **prude students** are **prudent**, since it's not a great idea to be 16 and pregnant.

puerile (adjective): childish. "PURE ul"

Think: **puberty**.

The high school freshman's **puerile** sense of humor was typical of a boy who was going through **puberty**.

pugnacious (adjective): wanting to fight. "pug NAY shus"

Think: **Pug nation**.

Imagine how **pugnacious** a **Pug nation** would be - those little dogs definitely would be fighting all the time.

pulchritude (noun): beauty. "PULK rih tude"

Think: **poll: Christ, dude**.

She had so much **pulchritude** that the most common response about her looks in the bros' **poll** was just, "**Christ, dude**!"

punctilious (adjective): marked by following the rules strictly. "punk TILL y-us"

Think: **punctual**.

The teacher's pet was both **punctilious** and **punctual**, but most wanted to punch him.

pungent (adjective): strongly scented. "PUN jent"

Think: **punch scent**.

The boxer's body odor was so **pungent** it was like getting hit by a **punch** of **scent**.

punitive (adjective): involving punishment.
"PYOON ih tive (rhymes with "give")"

Think: **punish**.

The **punitive** damages in the O.J. Simpson murder case were clearly designed to **punish** the defendant.

purist (noun): traditionalist, literalist. "PURE rissed"

Think: **pure wrist**.

I'm a **purist**, so I don't think you need a fancy set of titanium golf clubs to be a good golfer: a good golf swing is **pure wrist** and hips.

pusillanimous (adjective): cowardly.
"pyoo suh LAN ih-muss"

Think: **pussycat**.

The **pussycat** is an animal that is **pusillanimous** when scared - hence the expression "scaredy-cat".

putrid (adjective): foul or rotten. "PYOO trid"

Think: **puked**.

The dead mouse smelled so **putrid** that I almost **puked** while getting rid of it.

quagmire (noun): a difficult situation.
"KWAG mire (rhymes with "fire")"

Think: **quicksand mire**.

Quicksand can **mire** you if you step in it, and the more you struggle, the worse the **quagmire** becomes.

quail (verb): to pull back in fear. "kwale"

Think: **quail** (the bird).

I feel bad for **quail** (noun) - those poor birds **quail** (verb) as soon as they see people because they're often hunted for sport.

quandary (noun): a situation that makes you confused about what to do. "kwan duh rye"

Think: **wandering**.

I'm **wandering** around aimlessly because I'm in a **quandary** about where to go next.

quash (verb): to completely stop from happening. "kwash"

Think: **squash**.

The best way to **quash** an invasion of ants in your kitchen is simple: **squash** them.

querulous (adjective): whiny; complaining.
"KWER uh luss"

Think: **quarrel us**.

We'd invite you over more, but you're so **querulous** that you always end up in a **quarrel** with **us**!

quiescent (adjective): at rest. "KWEE ess ent"

Think: **quiet**.

The hibernating bear was both **quiet** and **quiescent**.

quintessential (adjective): the most typical; the purest. "kwin teh SEN shull"

Think: **essential**.

Watching a Red Sox game at Fenway Park is **essential** to get the **quintessential** Boston experience.

quixotic (adjective): idealistic; impractical. "kwicks OT ick"

Think: **quick exotic**.

It's **quixotic** to think that you should earn some **quick** cash by becoming an **exotic** dancer.

quizzical (adjective): questioning; teasing. "KWIZ ih cull"

Think: **quizzing**.

When I started asking my date about the periodic table, her **quizzical** expression seemed to be **quizzing** me about why I'd brought up such an awkward topic.

quotidian (adjective): daily. "kwoh TID (rhymes with "did") y-en"

Think: **quota**.

The meter maid met her daily **quota** of parking tickets by her **quotidian** patrolling of the streets.

raconteur (noun): a good storyteller. "rack on TURR"

Think: **recount**.

Jack White named one of his bands The **raconteurs** because they were so good at **recounting** stories via song.

ragamuffin (noun): a dirty, poor person or child. "RAG a muffin"

Think: **rags** on **muffin**.

The **rags** on your little **muffin** make him look like a **ragamuffin** - shop at Baby Gap next time.

raiment (noun): clothing. "RAY ment"

Think: **rain meant**.

In the nudist colony, a forecast of **rain meant** they'd actually have to don some **raiment**.

ramification (noun): the result of an action or decision. "RAM if a CAY shun"

Think: **Dodge Ram**.

One **ramification** of trading in my Prius for a **Dodge Ram** is that I am spending a lot more money on gas.

rampant (adjective): widespread; uncontrolled.
"RAM pent"

Think: **rampage**.

If you're dumb enough to take bath salts, the destruction after your **rampage** will be **rampant**.

rancorous (adjective): hateful. "RAN kur us"

Think: Star Wars **rancor**.

In Return Of The Jedi, the **rancor** under Jabba The Hutt's palace is undoubtedly **rancorous** for having been imprisoned.

rankled (verb): irritated. "RAN kulled"

Think: **wrinkled**.

Tim Gunn told the "Project Runway" contestant to "make it work", so the **wrinkled** dress she made **rankled** him.

rapacious (adjective): greedy; predatory; ravenous.
"ruh PAY shus"

Think: **rapes us**.

The **rapacious** new tax law takes so much of our earnings that it effectively **rapes us**.

rapt (adjective): completely interested. "RAPPED"

Think: **wrapped**.

The audience was held **rapt** by the master violinist's performance; they were completely **wrapped** up in it.

rapturous (adjective): full of wonderful feelings; ecstatic. "RAP shur us"

Think: **raptor** saw **us**.

The **raptor** saw **us** being lowered into his cage and felt **rapturous** since he was hungry.

rarefied (adjective): lofty; reserved only for a select few. "RARE uh fied"

Think: **rare find**.

The truffle your pig dug up is a **rare find**, peasant - you dare not eat such a **rarefied** delicacy - save it for his Majesty.

rash (adjective): hasty; incautious. "RASH"

Think: **rash** (noun).

If you make the **rash** (adjective) decision to have unprotected sex with that NBA player, you might get a **rash** (noun).

raucous (adjective): noisy; disorderly. "RAW kus"

Think: **rocks us**.

The Beastie Boys' **raucous** track, "Fight For Your Right to Party", **rocks us**.

raze (verb): to completely destroy. "RAZE"

Think: **rays blaze**.

The powerful laser's **rays** are making a **blaze** that will **raze** the old building to make room for the new one.

readily (adjective): with preparation / enthusiasm. "RED il-ly"

Think: **ready**.

If you are **ready** to answer a question, then you can answer it **readily**.

realization (noun): the making of something into reality. "Real liz a shun"

Think: **real Z nation.**

After a grueling, 15-year guerrilla war against the ruling forces of Rhodesia and its conservative white minority, the **nation** of Zimbabwe officially became independent in 1980, the **realization** of a longtime dream for independence.

reap (verb): to gather or obtain. "REEP"

Think: Grim **Reaper**.

If there's a knock on the door and you see the Grim **Reaper** through the peephole, don't answer: he has come to **reap** your life.

rebuttal (noun): a response. "re BUTT ul"

Think: **butt**.

After I lectured the college sophomore about the dangers of binge drinking, his **rebuttal** was to moon me – he showed me his **butt**.

recalcitrant (adjective): difficult to manage or change. "ruh CAL sih trant"

Think: **calc rant**.

The **calc** worksheet made Alex **rant** because it was so **recalcitrant**.

recant (verb): to formally deny a former position. "RE cant"

Think: **really I can't**.

I know I said I would move to Canada if we elected Obama, but **really I can't**, so I **recant** that statement.

recapitulated (verb): summarized. "RE kuh PIT u lated"

Think: **recap**.

His **recap** of the news nicely **recapitulated** the day's events.

recidivist (noun): someone who relapsed into crime. "ruh SID uh vist"

Think: **Sid's division**.

Sid had two sides to his personality: the law-abiding side and the **recidivist**.

reclusive (adjective): characterized by hiding and avoiding society. "ruh CLUE sive"

Think: brown **recluse**.

Luckily for us, the deadly poisonous brown **recluse** spider is **reclusive**.

recondite (adjective): not easily understood. "REH cun dite"

Think: **reckoned it**.

I couldn't understand my professor's **recondite** lecture, but I **reckoned it** had something to do with the fourth dimension.

recrudescent (adjective): reactivating. "reh kru DES sent"

Think: **recruits sent**.

The conflict in Afghanistan must be **recrudescent** since more **recruits** are **sent** there daily.

rectitude (noun): extreme integrity. "RECK tih tude"

Think: **correct attitude**.

Since he was a church rector, Paul considered the **correct attitude** to be **rectitude**.

redouble (verb): to greatly increase the size or amount of something. "re DUB ull"

Think: **double.**

Football practice was brutal today! Coach made us **double** our efforts, but then that wasn't enough for him, so we had to **redouble** them.

redress: to set right. "ruh DRESS"

Think: **re-dress** Lady Gaga.

Lady Gaga's fashion choices are so wrong that the only way to **redress** her style is to literally **re-dress** her.

reductive (adjective): related to making something smaller or simpler. "ruh DUCT ihve"

Think: **reduce.**

Reductive Spark Notes **reduce** brilliant works of literature into basic summaries.

redundant (adjective): needlessly repetitive.
"ruh DUN dent"

Think: **re-done.**

Duh... that has already been done well - it will be **redundant** if you decide it needs to be **redone.**

refracted (verb): distorted or changed from an initial direction. "re FRAK tid"

Think: **reflected fractured**.

The prism **refracted** the white light and **reflected** it, **fractured**, into a rainbow of colors.

refractory (adjective): stubborn; unmanageable. "ruh FRAK turry"

Think: **re-fracture**.

The **refractory** athlete insisted on playing despite his broken toe; unsurprisingly, he **re-fractured** it.

refulgent (adjective): brightly shining. "ruh FOOL jent"

Think: **refuels it**.

The campfire gets **refulgent** after he **refuels it**.

refute (verb): to speak against or disprove. "ruh FYOOT"

Think: **refuse**.

My dog **refutes** my argument that he needs a bath by adamantly **refusing** to get in the tub.

rejuvenated (verb): gave new life to. "ruh JUVE in ated"

Think: **re-juvenile**.

His plans for the new year **rejuvenated** the middle-aged man so much that he felt like a **juvenile** again.

relinquish (verb): to give up to or return to.
"ruh LEN quish"

Think: **release anguish**.

When I went to prison, I had to **relinquish** my baby boy to social services which gave me **release anguish**.

relish (verb): to enjoy; to savor. "REH lish"

Think: **delish**.

I **relish** (verb) eating hot dogs with **relish** (noun) because they taste **delish**.

remedial (adjective): intended to correct at a basic level. "ruh MEED y ul"

Think: **remedy**.

If you are terrible at math, the only **remedy** might be to take a **remedial** arithmetic class.

reminiscent (adjective): similar to, evoking.
"rem (rhymes with "gem") in IS int"

Think: **remind scent**.

The smell of baking bread is **reminiscent** of my youth; the
scent reminds me of my grandmother's kitchen.

remiss (adjective): careless. "ruh MISS"

Think: **re-miss**.

If you are **remiss** in your study technique, you'll miss the
point the first time you read then **re-miss** it the 2nd time.

remunerated (verb): compensated or paid for.
"ruh MOON ur ated"

Think: **re-moneyed**.

It cost me $300 to remove the rat from my apartment, but
my landlord **remunerated** / **"re-moneyed"** me.

renowned (adjective): famous in a good way.
"ruh NOUNED"

Think: **re-known**.

Renowned celebrities are often **known** in their era then
re-known on reality T.V. shows several years later.

276

repertoire (noun): "bag of tricks," canon.
"ryep uh TWAR"

Think: **repeat**.

When I followed the Grateful Dead around for a summer, I realized their **repertoire** was finite; their set list **repeated** most of the time.

replete (adjective): full. "ruh PLEET"

Think: **replace completely**.

Replace your energy **completely** after your workout so your body stays **replete** with energy.

reprehensible (adjective): deserving blame.
"rep ree HEN sih bull"

Think: **pretend hens**.

Heyyy... you sold me **pretend hens** instead of real ones - that's **reprehensible**.

reprobate (adjective): evil. "REP roh bait"

Think: **re-probed it**.

The aliens who gave Cartman an anal probe on "South Park" would be even more **reprobate** if they **re-probed it**.

reprove (verb): to gently criticize or correct. "reh PROVE"

Think: **reps at the gym.**

Some bodybuilder types can't help but **reprove** everyone else's technique while they doing **reps** at the gym.

repudiate (verb): to refuse to accept; to reject. "ruh PYOO dee ate"

Think: **refuse poo I ate.**

If I were to eat poo, my stomach would **refuse** the **poo I ate** and **repudiate** it by vomiting uncontrollably.

repugnant (adjective): gross. "ruh PUG nent"

Think: **ugly Pug.**

Although some people think **Pugs'** upturned faces and wheezing are cute, many find the breed to be **repugnant**.

requisite (adjective): necessary. "RECK wiz it"

Think: **requires it.**

If you fail English, your school **requires it** to be re-taken; it's **requisite** that you have four years of English.

resigned (adjective): reluctantly accepting of a bad situation. "ruh ZINED"

Think: **resignation**.

After being implicated in Watergate, Nixon was **resigned** and offered his **resignation** from office.

resilient (adjective): sturdy; flexible. "ruh ZILL y ent"

Think: **Brazil nut**.

Have you ever tried to crack open a **Brazil nut**? Their shells are **resilient**!

resolute (adjective): firmly determined. "rez oh LOOT"

Think: **resolution**.

It's no use to make a New Year's **resolution** if you're not **resolute** enough to follow through with it.

resonant (adjective): creating sonic vibrations (literal), connecting on a deep level (metaphorical). "REZ uh nent"

Think: **resin on it**.

Not only is Nina Simone's voice literally **resonant**, with a booming force that can stun a live crowd, but it is also figuratively **resonant** in that she is able to form a deep connection with her audience. Simone can sing or with as much grace or grit as the occasion requires, with the ability to take her usual tone and sprinkle some **resin on it**.

respite (adjective): a short rest. "RESS pit"

Think: **rest it**.

Don't overwork your respiratory system; if you take a **respite** and **rest it**, your lungs will thank you.

resplendent (adjective): shining brilliantly. "re SPLEN dint"

Think: **splendid**.

Cinderella was **resplendent** in a sequined, white ball gown; she looked absolutely **splendid**.

restitution (noun): the act of making up for something bad. "rest ih TOO shun"

Think: **rest** of **tuition**.

My college's **restitution** for allowing prostitution was paying the **rest** of our **tuition**.

restive (adjective): restless; fidgety.
"rest ive (rhymes with "give")"

Think: **rest** on **stove**.

Good luck taking a **rest** on a **stove** - you'll feel too **restive** to sleep because you'll worry it will turn on.

resurgence (noun): a comeback. "ruh SURGE ince"

Think: **re-surge**.

When LL Cool J said, "Don't call it a comeback", he meant that his **re-surging** to the top wasn't a **resurgence**.

reticent (adjective): reserved; quiet. "RET uh sent"

Think: **ready** but **hesitant**.

If you have to recite a speech and you're technically **ready** but **hesitant**, you might be **reticent**.

retiring (adjective): shy. "re TIRE ing"

Think: **retire** from parties.

The shy girl was so **retiring** that she decided that she would **retire** from going to parties.

retrenchment (noun): a reduction. "ruh TRENCH ment"

Think: **return** to **trench**.

For a WWI soldier, a **retrenchment** of the attack plans meant he could **return** to his **trench** and lay low for a while.

retrospection (noun): the act of thinking about the past. "reh tro SPEC shun"

Think: **retro-inspection**.

Retrospection about the 1980s is a **retro-inspection** that can lead to wearing neon clothes and leg warmers.

revamp (verb): to revise, improve, or make over. "re VAMP"

Think: return as a **vampire**.

If you're sucked dry by a **vampire**, don't worry - you'll die, but then be **revamped** as a strong, new member of the undead.

revanche (noun): revenge. "RE van shay"

Think: **revenge**.

Motivated by **revenge**, the French monarch ordered her general to take **revanche** on those who had captured the island.

reverberate (verb): to echo. "ruh VERB er ate"

Think: **re-vibrate**.

I yodeled in the empty concert hall, and the echoes **reverberated** and **re-vibrated** as they bounced off the walls.

reverent (adjective): having deep respect for. "REV ur ent"

Think: **reverend**.

During church, the **reverend** reminded them to be **reverent** to Jesus.

revile (verb): to abuse verbally. "ruh VILE"

Think: **evil, vile**.

My disillusionment with the army began when I tripped, causing the drill sergeant to **revile** me with the most **evil, vile** insults I've ever heard.

revulsion (noun): disgust. "ruh VUL shun"

Think: **revolt** and **shun**.

When the king barfed then ate the barf, I felt such **revulsion** that I wanted to **revolt** and **shun** him.

rhapsodize (verb): to enthusiastically praise. "RAP sa dyes"

Think: **rapture**.

The rapper Sisqo felt so much **rapture** when looking at women wearing thongs that he **rhapsodized** about them in "The Thong Song".

rhetorical (adjective): hypothetical, related to rhetoric (communication style). "rhuh TORE ih cull"

Think: **Slick Rick's rhetoric**.

Rapper **Slick Rick** is a smooth talker; in other words, he has **slick rhetoric**.

rickety (adjective): weak. "RIK it y"

Think: **rickets**.

Rickets, a disease that weakens the bones, makes its sufferers **rickety**.

rift (noun): a break or split. "RIFT"

Think: **ripped.**

The **rift** in our friendship was so deep that it felt as though our bond had been **ripped.**

riposte (noun): a comeback. "rih PAWST"

Think: **rip post.**

After being mocked, the blogger would **rip** into his critic's **post** with a brutal **riposte.**

risible (adjective): funny; inclined to laugh. "RIZ uh bull"

Think: get a **rise.**

If you like to get a **rise** out of people by being a class clown, you're probably **risible.**

risque (adjective): almost improper or indecent. "riss K"

Think: **risky.**

Making a **risque** joke the first time you meet your girlfriend's parents is **risky.**

roborant (noun): an invigorating drug. "ROB uh rent"

Think: **robo-ant**.

After I gave him a **roborant**, my ant felt as strong as a **robo-ant**.

robust (adjective): healthy; strong; rich; full. "roh BUST"

Think: **robots**.

Humans wouldn't last long on Mars due to the extreme cold - we sent **robots** since they're more **robust**.

rotund (adjective): round; full; plump. "roh TUND"

Think: **round tummy**.

Your pet hippo's **tummy** has grown so **rotund** that it's literally **round** at this point.

row (noun): a disagreement. "ROW (rhymes with "plow")"

Think: **rrrr...ow!**

The **row** between the two boys started with growling: "**rrrr!**" and was quickly followed by an "**ow!**" as one punched the other.

rudimentary (adjective): basic; primitive.
"rude ih MENT uh ry"

Think: **rude elementary**.

Rude elementary school kids are impolite only because their knowledge of social graces is **rudimentary**.

ruffian (noun): a brutal person. "RUFFY en"

Think: **rough**.

The club hired a **ruffian** as a bouncer because he was strong enough to be **rough** with misbehaving drunks.

ruminate (verb): to carefully reflect on. "ROOM in ate"

Think: **Ramen marinate**.

To **ruminate** means to think about something for at least as long as it takes your Top **Ramen** to **marinate**.

saccharine (adjective): sweet in a fake way. "SACK a rin"

Think: **saccharin**.

The beauty contestant's personality was so **saccharine** that there must have been Sweet and Low (**saccharin**) in her veins.

sacrosanct (adjective): holy. "SACK ro SANKED"

Think: **sacred sanctuary**.

The temple was a **sacred sanctuary** and was declared **sacrosanct** to protect it from real estate developers.

salacious (adjective): appealing to sexual desire. "suh LA shus"

Think: **salivate**.

All the girls read *Fifty Shades of Gray* because the **salacious** details make them **salivate**.

salient (adjective): very important or noticeable. "SAY lee ent"

Think: **saline**.

If you're dehydrated, getting **saline** into your bloodstream is your most **salient** concern.

salubrious (adjective): good for your health. "Sal OOH bree us"

Think: **salute.**

The kale smoothie I just drank was so **salubrious** that my stomach would **salute** me if it could.

salutary (adjective): beneficial.
"SAL (rhymes with "pal") u tary"

Think: **salute**.

Sal's cooking has such a **salutary** effect on me that I **salute** him.

sangfroid (noun): coolness and composure.
"sang FRWA (it's a French word)"

Think: **sang frog**.

"You don't scare me!" **sang** the **frog** when he saw the fox - he had **sangfroid** in spades.

sanguine (adjective): optimistic. "SAN gwin"

Think: Penguin **sang win**.

The penguin **sang** that he would **win**; he was **sanguine**.

sap (verb): to weaken. "SAP"

Think: tree **sap**.

Cutting your initials into a tree can **sap** (verb) its vitality because it will make the **sap** (noun) leak out.

sapid (adjective): flavorful. "SAP id"

Think: maple **sap**.

We make maple syrup from the **sap** of maple trees because their **sap** is naturally **sapid**.

sapient (adjective): wise. "SAP y ent"

Think: *Homo sapiens*.

Be proud that you're a member of *Homo sapiens*; you're more **sapient** than any other animal on the planet.

sardonic (adjective): mocking (in a mean way). "sar DON ick"

Think: **sarcastic sardines**.

When the seniors saw I ate **sardines** for lunch every day, they made **sardonic**, **sarcastic** comments.

sashayed (verb): strutted or walked in a showy or flashy way. "sah SHAYED"

Think: Miss America **sash**.

Miss America **sashayed** across the stage, showing off her first-place **sash**.

satiated (adjective): satisfied. "SAY she ated"

Think: **say she ate**.

If you **say she ate**, she must be **satiated**.

scanty (adjective): barely sufficient; minimal. "SKAN tee"

Think: **scanty panty**.

Thong underwear is basically just a really **scanty panty**.

scapegoat (noun): one that takes the blame. "SKAPE goat"

Think: **escaped goat**.

Even though the dog ate some of the vegetables in the garden, the **escaped goat** became the **scapegoat**.

scathing (adjective): sharply critical. "SKAY thing"

Think: **scythe**.

Getting killed by the Grim Reaper's sharp, hooked **scythe** is as about as **scathing** a criticism as one can get.

schadenfreude (noun): enjoyment from others' troubles. "SHA den froy dah"

Think: **shady Freud**.

If your psychologist giggles about your divorce he has **schadenfreude** and is a **shady Freud**.

schism (noun): a separation into opposing groups; a divide. "skism"

Think: **schizophrenic**.

The **schizophrenic** patient underwent a **schism** that gave him multiple personalities.

scintillating (adjective): sparkling; brilliant. "SIN tull ating"

Think: **squint**.

Her sequined shirt was so **scintillating** that I had to **squint** to see it.

sclerotic (adjective): rigid; reluctant to adapt or compromise. "sclear OTT ick"

Think: **arthosclerosis**.

When plaque builds up inside someone's arteries, he can develop **arthosclerosis** – a dangerous condition in which those blood vessels become **sclerotic**.

scofflaw (noun): a contemptuous law-breaker. "SKOF law"

Think: **scoff** at the **law**.

A **scofflaw** will **scoff** at the **law** he just broke since he has no respect for it.

scotch (verb): to put a sudden end to; to injure. "Skotch"

Think: **scratch**.

Well, the boss just **scotched** our plan to bring our cats to work, so **scratch** that idea.

scrupulous (adjective): having integrity, or being exact. "SKRUP u luss"

Think: **scrape** the **poop**.

If you are **scrupulous**, you will **scrape** your dog's **poop** off my lawn.

scrutinize (verb): to examine carefully. "SKROO tin eyes"

Think: desire to **screw in eyes**.

I'm an 18-year-old cheerleader - when a dirty old man **scrutinizes** me, I see the desire to **screw in** his **eyes**.

scuffle (noun): a brief fight. "SKUFF ul"

Think: **scuff**.

The **scuffle** was no big deal, but I did **scuff** my new pair of shoes.

scurrilous (adjective): obscenely abusive. "SKURR a lus"

Think: **scurvy curses**.

After the pirate developed **scurvy**, his **curses** became even more **scurrilous**.

scuttle (verb): to destroy; to scrap. "SKUT ul"

Think: **it's cut**.

Scuttle the launch of that Space Shuttle! **It's cut** from the space program as of 2011.

secretes (verb): forms and gives off. "suh CREETS"

Think: **secret sea creature**.

The octopus is a **sea creature** that stays **secret** when it **secretes** an inky cloud.

sectarian (adjective): narrow-minded. "sek TEAR y-en"

Think: **sector**.

Sectarian views are shallow because they only consider one **sector** of the whole issue.

secular (adjective): not related to the spiritual or religious. "SEK u lur"

Think: **sex u later**.

"If ur religious, I am not interested, but if ur **secular** I might want to **sex you later**," said the poorly written Tinder profile.

sedentary (adjective): inactive; lazy. "suh DENT a ry"

Think: **sofa dent**.

Sedentary people make **sofa dents** because they sit on the cushions for hours at a time.

sedulous (adjective): careful; hardworking; diligent.
"SED u lus"

Think: **schedule us**.

Our **sedulous** hairstylist is always able to **schedule us** since she's so efficient.

segue (noun): a transition. "seg WAY"

Think: **Segway**.

A good way to make sure your friends go along with your conversational **segue** is to barge in riding a **Segway**.

self-styled (adjective): self-proclaimed. "Self-sty-ulled"

Think: **selfie style.**

The Kardashians are **self-styled** experts on fashion as evidenced by how many **selfies** they take of their **style**.

semblance (noun): an outward appearance; an image. "sem BLENSE"

Think: **resemblance**.

The lie fooled me because it had the **semblance** of honesty, a slight **resemblance** to the truth.

seminal (adjective): important; original. "SEM in ul"

Think: **seminar**.

If a book is **seminal**, you're probably gonna have to read it in your freshman year literature **seminar**.

sententious (adjective): using quotable or preachy sayings. "sen TEN shus"

Think: **sentences**.

The Reverend Jesse Jackson is **sententious** because many people quote his **sentences**.

sentient (adjective): having sense perception; conscious. "SENTY ent"

Think: **sensed it**.

I knew the alien life form was **sentient** after I pricked it with a pin and it moved: it **sensed it**.

sequacious (adjective): something that imitates another's idea. "suh QUAY shus"

Think: **sequel**.

Your movie is so **sequacious** of mine that it feels like a **sequel**.

sere (adjective): dried; withered. "SEER"

Think: **sear**.

If you **sear** those vegetables on the grill too long they'll become **sere**.

serendipity (noun): luck. "ser en DIP ih tee"

Think: **Sara ended pity**.

After winning the lottery, **Sara ended** her **pity** toward herself because of her amazing **serendipity**.

servile (adjective): submissive. "sir VILE"

Think: **servant**.

The **servant** was so **servile** that he wouldn't make eye contact.

sham (noun): a trick that deceives. "SHAM"

Think: **shame**.

Your story about being a doctor is a **sham**...**shame** on you!

shard (noun): a broken piece of something fragile. "SHARD"

Think: **sharp**.

Be careful of the **shard** of glass on the floor; it's really **sharp**.

shelve (verb): to put aside or postpone. "SHELVE"

Think: **shelf**.

I **shleved** my plan to sabotage my rival and put my notes for it back on the **shelf** once I learned I got the promotion.

shirk (verb): to avoid a duty. "SHIRK"

Think: **shark**.

If the beach lifeguard **shirks** his duties, then you might want to keep a look out for **sharks**.

showy (adjective): designed to attract attention. "SHOWY"

Think: **show**.

Donald Trump's **showy**, gold-plated toilet was clearly designed to **show** off his wealth.

shrewd (adjective): clever. "SHROOD"

Think: **sued**.

The **shrewd** attorney **sued** as many people as she could; she knew her superior knowledge of the law would make her win.

simper (verb): to smile in a silly way. "SIMPER"

Think: **smile chimp**.

Have you ever seen a **smile** on a **chimp**? They **simper** in a way that cracks me up.

simulacrum (noun): an image or representation of something. "sim u LAY crum"

Think: **simulation**.

Coachella audiences saw a **simulacrum** of Tupac: a hologram that was an incredible **simulation** of him.

sinuous (adjective): having many curves. "SIN u is"

Think: **sine wave**.

Unsurprisingly, if you graph a **sine** wave on your calculator it's going to look **sinuous**.

skittish (adjective): restless; easily frightened. "SKIT ish"

Think: **Skittles**.

After I ate a 54 oz. bag of **Skittles** by myself, the sugar high made me **skittish**.

skulduggery (noun): tricky or sneaky behavior. "skul DUG er y"

Think: **skull** he **dug**.

The **skull** he **dug** up from the local cemetery proved he was a witch doctor who practiced **skulduggery**.

skulk (verb): to hide or be stealthy. "SKULK"

Think: **skunks lurk**.

Skunks lurk and **skulk** until it's dark enough for them to eat from your garbage cans.

slake (verb): to quench or satisfy. "SLAKE"

Think: **lake**.

If you're a zebra, you probably can't operate a water fountain: **slake** your thirst at the **lake**.

slander (noun): a false statement intended to hurt someone's reputation. "SLAN der"

Think: **slammed her.**

To try to steal voters from Hillary Clinton, Donald Trump repeatedly **slammed her** in interviews, figuring that enough **slander** against her might make voters forget how deplorable he was.

slatternly (adjective): untidy or promiscuous. "SLA tern ly"

Think: **slutty.**

If you want to say she's **slutty** but use a bit more flattery, call her **slatternly**.

slipshod (adjective): careless; sloppy. "SLIP shod"

Think: **slip shoddy.**

I **slip** when I walk on your **shoddy** living room floor because its construction is really **slipshod**.

slothful (adjective): lazy. "SLOTH ful"

Think: **sloth.**

My pet **sloth** is too **slothful** to move even when he's really hungry.

slovenly (adjective): untidy; sloppy. "SLOV en lee"

Think: **sloppy.**

Charlie Brown's friends make fun of Pig-Pen because of his **sloppy, slovenly** appearance.

sojourn (noun): a temporary stay. "SO jern"

Think: **journey.**

If you **journey** somewhere, it's probably for a **sojourn** unless you bought a one-way ticket.

solecism (noun): a blunder. "SO luh sism"

Think: **sole is in.**

If you put your foot in your mouth - like if you ask a woman her age - it's a **solecism** - your **sole is in** your mouth.

solicitous (adjective): concerned for. "so LISS it us"

Think: **solely listened to us.**

I knew the man was **solicitous** because he **solely listened to us**.

solidarity (adjective): unity, agreement, mutual support. "Solid AIR ity"

Think: **solid dare.**

Normally, I'm not one to accept a **dare**, but due to our **solid** friendship and **solidarity**, I will accept your challenge to run a marathon for charity.

solipsistic (adjective): being extremely self-centered. "sah lip SIS tick"

Think: **sold lipstick.**

The model whose image **sold lipstick** became **solipsistic** due to all the compliments she received.

somnolent (adjective): sleepy. "SAWM nuh lint"

Think: **insomnia.**

If you have **insomnia** you're probably **somnolent** from lack of sleep.

sonorous (adjective): having a deep, rich sound. "SAWN er us"

Think: **Tyranno-sonorous rex.**

Tyrannosaurus rex had a **sonorous** roar that could be heard for miles.

sophistry (noun): deceptive reasoning. "SO fis tree"

Think: **sophisticated trickery.**

Sophocles' **sophistry** was so **sophisticated** that his **trickery** made his character Oedipus kill his dad and marry his mom.

sophomoric (adjective): immature. "sof uh MOR ick"

Think: **sophomore-onic.**

Sophomores act **moronic** since they're immature and are more **sophomoric** than seniors.

soporific (adjective): causing sleep. "sop or IF ick"

Think: **sleepover-ific.**

That boring movie is perfect for our slumber party - it's **sleepover-ific** because it's **soporific.**

sordid (adjective): filthy; foul; morally degraded. "SORE did"

Think: **sorry I did.**

If you are a normal person with a conscience and you do something **sordid**, you'll be thinking, "**sorry I did** that" before long.

soupcon (noun): a little bit. "SOUP sawn"

Think: **soup can.**

After surviving the apocalypse, we only had a **soupcon** of food left: in fact, we only had one Campbell's **soup can.**

sovereign (adjective): independent. "SAW vern"

Think: **reign.**

If you're **sovereign**, you **reign** over your world and no one else does.

sparing (adjective): not using or giving a lot of something. "Spare ing"

Think: **spare ring.**

I'm a **sparing** guy, so when I proposed to my girlfriend, I asked her if she had a **spare ring** I could use as the engagement ring.

sparse (adjective): simple, unadorned, austere. "SPARSE"

Think: **sparks.**

When I saw how **simple** her apartment was, **sparks** flew: I have always been attracted to **minimalism.**

specious (adjective): seeming true but actually false. "SPEE shus"

Think: **suspicious** McLovin.

It's understandable the cashier in Superbad is **suspicious** when she sees Fogell's **specious** license that identifies him as "McLovin".

spendthrift (noun): someone who spends wastefully. "SPEND thrift"

Think: **spend** before **thrift**.

Spendthrift means someone for whom **spending** comes before being **thrifty**.

splenetic (adjective): bad-tempered. "spluh NET ick"

Think: **spleen** anger.

In medieval times, people thought anger came from one's **spleen**; "**splenetic**" was coined to describe an angry person.

spurious (adjective): false. "SPUR y us"

Think: **spur curious**.

His **spur**-of-the-moment explanation made me **curious** whether his story was **spurious**.

squalid (adjective): filthy. "SQUA lid"

Think: **squat lid**.

If the bathroom stall is **squalid**, **squat** over the **lid** when you pee.

squelch (verb): to crush or silence. "SKWELSH"

Think: **squash** and **squish**.

Squelch the ant uprising! **Squash** them! **Squish** them!

stalwart (adjective): loyal; strong supporter. "STAL wert"

Think: **tall war hero**.

George Washington was a **tall war** hero and all-around **stalwart**: he was a **strong, loyal supporter** of the American Revolution.

stanch (verb): to stop the flowing of. "STANCH"

Think: **'stache**.

I thought my **'stache** was sexy, but in fact it **stanched** the flow of all females to my bedroom.

staple (noun): something commonly used; an essential. "STA pull"

Think: **maple**.

At IHOP, **maple** syrup is a **staple** since they serve about a billion pancakes a year.

statuesque (adjective): attractively tall. "stah choo ESK"

Think: **statue** *Esquire*.

I wanted to make a **statue** of the *Esquire* model because she was so **statuesque**.

staunch (adjective): firm; true; strong. "STONCH"

Think: **stay unch**anged.

I'm a **staunch** supporter of Justin Bieber, so my support for him will **stay unchanged** even if he does something really stupid.

steadfast (adjective): loyal; immovable. "STEAD fast"

Think: **stayed fastened**.

The fallen soldier's dog was so **steadfast** that it **stayed fastened** to the ground near his grave.

stigmas (noun): marks of shame. "STIG mas"

Think: **Stick-mas** instead of Christmas.

One of our **stigmas** growing up was that we celebrated "**Stick-mas**" instead of Christmas – we were too poor for any presents but sticks.

stilted (adjective): overly formal; stiff. "STILL tid"

Think: **stilts**.

The soldier's manner of walking was so **stilted** that it looked like his legs were actually wooden **stilts**.

stolid (adjective): unemotional. "STOW lid"

Think: **solid**.

The **stolid** butler was **solid** and expressionless; he never broke down and cried.

storied (adjective): having an interesting/celebrated history. "STOH reed"

Think: **stories**.

The most interesting man in the world's **storied** history makes people tell his **stories**.

stratagem (noun): a clever scheme. "STRAT a gem"

Think: **strategy gem.**

The general's battlefield **strategy** was such a **gem** that most historians call it a **stratagem.**

streamlined (adjective): simplified; modernized. "STREAM lined"

Think: **stream line.**

The **streamlined** shape of a trout lets it swim through even a rushing **stream** in a straight **line.**

strenuous: (adjective): requiring lots of energy. "STREN u us"

Think: **strain on us.**

The **strenuous** hike up Mt. Whitney was a **strain on us.**

stricture (noun): a restraint; a criticism. "STRICT sure"

Think: **restrict.**

The tourniquet around my arm stopped me from bleeding to death, but the **stricture restricted** any circulation and they almost had to amputate my limb.

strident (adjective): harsh; loud. "STRI dent"

Think: **Stridex**.

Stridex commercials are as **strident** as the salicylic acid in the pads, in an effort to hold teens' interest.

stringent (adjective): strict. "STRIN jent"

Think: **strict gent**.

Our architecture professor is a **strict gent**: he's so **stringent** that if your drawing has any eraser marks, he'll dock you a full letter grade.

stultify (verb): to make ineffective. "STULT ih fy"

Think: **stupid dolt**.

If you **stultify** yourself by punching yourself in the skull, you'll become a **stupid dolt**.

stupefied (adjective): stunned. "STOOP uh fyed"

Think: **stupid**.

Hermione cast the **stupefy** spell on Crabbe, who became so **stupefied** that he looked **stupid**.

312

subjective (adjective): personal; unaffected by the outside world. "sub JEKT ive"

Think: king's **subject**.

His Majesty considers me to be his **subject** and his **subjective** opinion is that I'm a peasant even though I'm of noble birth.

sublime (adjective): awesome. "sub LIME"

Think: the band "**Sublime**".

The band **Sublime** has spawned several cover bands, a good sign that it made **sublime** music.

subsequent (adjective): following, next. "SUB suh kwent"

Think: **sub-sequence = next in the sequence.**

A **subsequence** is the **next** occurrence in a sequence: **that which follows**.

subsidy (noun): government aid to keep a price low. "SUB sih dee"

Think: **sub city**.

In order to prevent itself from becoming a **sub-city** in the wake of its bankruptcy, the city of Detroit had to rely on **subsidies** from the federal government.

substantiate (verb): to support with proof or evidence. "sub STANCH ee ate"

Think: **substance**.

You won't be able to **substantiate** your claim that I ate your lunch without evidence that has more **substance**.

subversive (adjective): seeking to undermine or disturb. "sub VERSE ive"

Think: **subversive verses**.

The political poet was detained by government officials for her "**subversive verses**."

subvert (verb): to weaken or ruin. "sub VERT"

Think: **sub hurt**.

Captain: the torpedo from that **sub hurt** our ship and **subverted** our morale.

succor (noun): aid. "SUCK er"

Think: **supper**.

If you're starving and stranded in a snowstorm, hopefully your **succor** will include some sort of **supper**.

succumb (verb): to give in to a superior force. "suh KUM"

Think: **suck under**.

Do not **succumb** to the deadly pull of the quicksand or it will **suck** you **under**.

sullen (adjective): sad, gloomy, resentful. "SULL en"

Think: **mullet**.

The barber gave me a **mullet** – that's why I'm so **sullen**.

sumptuary (adjective): made to prevent overindulgence. "SUMP tyoo air y"

Think: **consumption-ary**.

Consumption of harmful things, like cigarettes or alcohol, can be limited with a **sumptuary** tax.

superficial (adjective): on the surface. "soup er FISH ul"

Think: **super official website**.

The shiny new website for the family restaurant looked **super official**, but the truth was that it was starving for customers: so far, the success of the business was only **superficial**.

supplant (verb): replace. "suh PLANT"

Think: **up plant**.

After you pull **up** a **plant** out of the soil, you should **supplant** it with another one to help preserve the environment.

surly (adjective): in a foul mood, ill-tempered. "SUR ly"

Think: **swirly**.

The school bully gave me a **swirly** (he stuck my head in a toilet and flushed it) – that's why I'm **surly**.

surmise (verb): to guess. "sur MISE"

Think: **summarize**.

Since a police report will only **summarize** what happened, one usually has to **surmise** the actual events of a crime.

surpassing (adjective): really, really great. "sur PASS ing"

Think: **super pass**.

If you're **super** at running, you'll **pass** everyone due to your **surpassing** speed.

surreptitious (adjective): sneaky or stealthy. "sur ep TISH us"

Think: **reptiles**.

Reptiles like snakes are good at camouflage because they're **surreptitious**.

susceptible (adjective): easily affected or influenced by something. "suh SEPT ih bull"

Think: **suggest-able**.

I'm **susceptible** to pranks because I'm so **suggest-able** – I'll follow any suggestion.

swathe (noun, verb) a cover or wrap / to cover or wrap. "SWAYTHE"

Think: **swat the (mosquitos)**.

When camping near standing water, I would rather **swathe** myself in mosquito repellent than **swat the** pesky pests away all day.

sybarite (noun): one devoted to pleasure. "SIB a right"

Think: **sit** at a **bar**.

If you go **sit** at a **bar** every night to watch sports and drink beer, you might be a **sybarite**.

sycophant (noun): one who flatters for self gain.
"SICK a fent"

Think: **sick of elephant**.

The animals were **sick of** the **elephant** because he was a
sycophant who kissed up to the zookeeper.

synergy (noun): combined action that produces mutually
helpful results. "SIN ur gee"

Think: **'N SYNC energy**.

By forming a boy band and using **synergy**, **'N SYNC** created
more **energy** than they would had they all gone solo.

synoptic (adjective): giving a summary. "sin OP tick"

Think: **synopsis**.

The **synoptic** nature of SparkNotes provides a **synopsis** of
a novel's plot at the expense of the novel's beauty.

syntax (noun): linguistics, use of language. "SIN tax"

Think: **sin tax**.

The conservative legislature once tried to impose a "**sin
tax**" on all gay marriages, but was forced to change its
syntax due to a lawsuit from the ACLU.

taciturn (adjective): not talkative. "TASS it turn"

Think: **takes his turn**.

If she's passive and **taciturn** at the debate and just politely **takes her turn** when speaking, she'll never win.

tangible (adjective): able to be touched. "TAN jib ul"

Think: **tango-ble**.

If you can dance the **tango** with someone – if she's **tango-ble** – then she's perforce **tangible**.

taxonomic (adjective): related to the process of categorization. "Taks oh NOM ik"

Think: **taxes are not my thing**.

Because I am a creative type, doing my **taxes** each year, along with all the requisite **classifications and categorizations** of various personal and business expenses, is a **taxonomic** activity that is clearly **not my thing**. Time to hire an accountant.

temerity (noun): recklessness.
"tuh MERR (rhymes with "err") uh tee"

Think: **team error**.

If you have **temerity**, maybe you should join **team error** because I bet you make a lot of mistakes.

temperance (noun): moderation. "TEM per ence"

Think: **temper ants**.

At the picnic, I didn't lose my **temper** over the **ants**, because I possess the quality of **temperance**.

tempestuous (adjective): stormy. "tem PEST you us"

Think: **tempers**.

Our hot **tempers** make **us** have a **tempestuous** relationship.

temporal (adjective): relating to time. "TEM puh rull"

Think: **temporary**.

Technically, diamonds aren't forever; in a **temporal** sense, they're only **temporary** and will turn to dust one day.

tenable (adjective): able to be defended; workable. "TEN uh bull"

Think: **ten able.**

The scientist's theory was **tenable** because it was "**ten-able**", worthy of being rated a 10 out of 10.

tendentious (adjective): biased. "ten DEN shus"

Think: **tendency.**

Don't let him judge the beauty contest: he's **tendentious** and has a **tendency** to vote for the contestants that flirt with him the most.

tensile (adjective): related to tension. "TENSE I'll"

Think: **dense tile.**

The **tensile** strength of that **dense** old **tile** on the kitchen counter is quite impressive, which is why I've been having such a hard time removing it during renovations.

tenuous (adjective): lacking substance or strength. "TEN you us"

Think: **tentative.**

At the debate, the **tentative** speaker's argument was unsurprisingly judged to be **tenuous**.

tepid (adjective): lukewarm, apathetic. "TEH pid"

Think: **"tap it" = tap the tepid keg**.

"Should I tap this keg now?" asked the overzealous fraternity brother. "Um, sure, I guess you could **tap it**" was my **tepid** response: it was full of **tepid** beer.

terse (adjective): brief and abrupt. "TURSE"

Think: **terse verse**.

Haikus are **verses** / That are as **terse** as the lives / Of gentle fruit flies.

timorous (adjective): fearful. "TIM uh riss"

Think: **timid of us**.

Tim felt **timid** around **us** since he was **timorous**.

tirade (noun): a long angry speech. "TIE raid"

Think: **tired** of **rage**.

If someone gives you a **tirade**, you'll probably be **tired** of the **rage** after a few minutes.

titular (adjective): relating to a title. "TITCH u lur"

Think: **title**.

The **titular** character in *Harry Potter* is Harry Potter because his name is also the **title** of the book.

tonic (noun): something helpful. "TAWN ick"

Think: gin and **tonic**.

Drinking a gin and **tonic** before my speech was a **tonic** for my anxiety.

toothsome (adjective): tasty; appealing. "TOOTH some"

Think: **tooth some**.

The food looked so **toothsome** that I wanted to give my **tooth some**.

torpid (adjective): sluggish. "TOR pid"

Think: **tar pit**.

Once I walked into the sticky **tar pit**, my pace became **torpid**.

tortuous (adjective): winding. "TOR tyoo us"

Think: **tortoise**.

The streets of Boston are so **tortuous** that you have to drive at **tortoise's** speed.

totalitarian (adjective): relating to a government with total power. "TOE tal (rhymes with "gal") ih TEAR y en"

Think: **total** power.

Our **totalitarian** dictator uses his **total** power to make us eat **Total** cereal daily - he's a control freak.

touted (verb): praised publicly. "TOUT ed"

Think: **shouted**.

Guinness Stout is highly **touted**; I know this because the guy drinking it next to me **shouted** its praises in my ear.

tranquil (adjective): calm. "TRAN quil"

Think: **NyQuil**.

Taking **NyQuil** before bed made me so **tranquil** that I slept for 12 hours.

transgression (noun): a violation of a rule.
"TRANS gression"

Think: **trans aggression.**

Some states have passed laws that make using a bathroom different than your biological gender a **transgression** due to fear of **trans aggression.**

transitory (adjective): existing only briefly.
"TRANS ih tory"

Think: **transit story.**

I found romance on the subway, but alas, our love was **transitory**: it was a public **transit story** that only lasted until her stop.

treacly (adjective): overly sweet or sentimental.
"TREAK (rhymes with leak) lee"

Think: **trickle-y** tears.

The scene with a homeless puppy is so **treacly** it seems designed to make tears **trickle** down one's face.

tremulous (adjective): fearful. "TREM you luss"

Think: **tremble**.

I felt so **tremulous** when I saw a shark swim underneath me that I began to **tremble**.

trepidation (noun): fear. "treh pid AY shun"

Think: **trap**.

The haunted house filled me with **trepidation**; I feared a **trap** would be sprung on me at any moment.

trifling (adjective): unimportant, inconsequential. "TRY fling"

Think: **rifling through drawers**.

If shadowy henchmen are **rifling through your drawers** for some reason, then it's probably more than a **trifling** matter.

truculent (adjective): ready to fight. "TRUCK you lent"

Think: **truce you lent**.

The armies should write their own peace treaty, because they're still **truculent** after that **truce you lent** them.

truncated (adjective): shortened. "TRUN kated"

Think: **trunk ate**.

The elephant's **trunk ate** so many branches that the tree was **truncated**.

tumid (adjective): swollen. "TYOO mid"

Think: **tumor-ed**.

The cancer patient's large **tumor** caused his abdomen to be **tumid**.

tumultuous (adjective): disorderly; like a riot.
"tuh MULT you us"

Think: **tumbled us**.

The mosh pit was so **tumultuous** that it **tumbled us** around like a dryer.

turbid (adjective): stirred up and made unclear or muddy.
"TURR (rhymes with "purr") bid"

Think: **tar bed**.

The lake became **turbid** when storms disturbed particles from the **tar bed** underneath its waters.

turgid (adjective): swollen.
"TURR (rhymes with "purr") jid"

Think: **turkey in**.

After Thanksgiving dinner, my belly was so **turgid** that it looked like I had eaten the whole **turkey**.

turpitude (noun): vile or immoral behavior.
"TURP ih tude"

Think: **turd attitude**.

His **turd attitude** made him engage in **turpitude**.

ubiquitous (adjective): existing everywhere.
"ooh BICK quit us"

Think: **you big Quidditch**.

You big Quidditch fans have made the *Harry Potter* sport **ubiquitous** on college campuses.

umbrage (noun): offense; annoyance. "UM bridge"

Think: **umbrella rage**.

Someone who takes **umbrage** at his **umbrella** probably felt **rage** when it broke during a storm.

unadorned (adjective): plain. "un uh DORNED"

Think: **unadored.**

Since your girlfriend's hand has no ring and is **unadorned**, I assume she's **unadored**: if you like it then you should put a ring on it.

unassuming (adjective): modest. "un uh SOOM ing"

Think: **un-assume**.

The millionaire's **unassuming** car definitely didn't make us **assume** he was wealthy.

unbridled (adjective): not restrained.
"un BRIDE ulled (rhymes with "culled")"

Think: **un-bridle**.

After I took off my horse's **bridle**, he became so **unbridled** that I had no control over him.

unconscionable (adjective): unreasonable; not guided by conscience. "un CON shin uh bull"

Think: **un-conscience**.

It would be **unconscionable** to leave your two-year-old alone at home - you'd have to have no conscience - an "**un-conscience**".

unconventional (adjective): not typical.
"Un con VENT shin ull"

Think: Republican **Convention.**

The most **unconventional** thing about the Republican **Convention** was its candidate, Donald Trump.

unctuous (adjective): smooth in a fake way. "UNK shis"

Think: **skunk-tous.**

Pepe Le Pew, the smooth-talking, playboy **skunk**, acts **unctuous** to charm the ladies.

uncultivated (adjective): not grown or used, (of a person) not refined. "Un KULT iv ate id"

Think: **cult avoided.**

Because of his simple, **uncultivated** nature, he was, somewhat ironically, able to **avoid** the siren call of the radical **cult** that was full of "intelligent" people from his town.

undermine (verb): to weaken in a sneaky way. "UN der mine"

Think: **under mine**.

Under the ground lay a land **mine** designed to **undermine** the army's advance.

underscore (verb): to highlight. "UN der score"

Think: **to score = to write**.

To **score** a composition is to write a composition; to **underscore** something on a piece of paper, you **write under** it (underline).

understated (adjective): downplayed; made to seem less than it actually is. "UN der stated"

Think: **understatement**.

"I have no complaints" is an **understated** way to respond if you're wealthy and asked how much money you make; it's an **understatement**.

undulate (verb): to move in a smooth, wavelike way. "UN dyoo late"

Think: **undo lace**.

You'll definitely turn your lover on if you **undo** your **lace** lingerie while slowly **undulating** your body.

uniform (adjective): always the same. "YOON if orm"

Think: Army **uniform**.

Throughout the U.S., the **uniform** (noun) that Army soldiers wear is **uniform** (adjective).

unkempt (adjective): untidy. "un KEMT"

Think: **un-kept** hair.

If you had just **kept** up with your personal hygiene, your hair wouldn't be so **unkempt** and birds wouldn't have nested in it.

unpretentiousness (noun): the state of being unassuming, modest, or natural. "Un pree TEN shish niss"

Think: **un-pretend us Ness**.

Ness did **not** try to **pretend** to be more glamorous or important than she truly was around **us**; hence, we found her personality refreshing and **unpretentious**.

unpropitious (adjective): unfavorable, not a good sign or omen. "Un pruh PISH us".

Think: **un propped.**

Grandpa's crutches **prop** him up; it's **unpropitious** that they're lost, since he's now **un-propped** and might fall.

unruly (adjective): difficult to discipline or manage. "un RULE y"

Think: **un-rule-able**.

My two-year-old is **unruly**; he is **un-rule-able** and says "No!" to me every time I tell him to do something.

unsavory (adjective): unpleasant, esp. morally unpleasant. "un SAVE or y"

Think: **un-savor**.

The icky memory of the **unsavory** used car salesman was not one I wanted to **save** or **savor**.

untenable (adjective): not workable, indefensible, weak, shaky. "un TEN uh bull"

Think: **un tent-able.**

If you are stuck in the woods during a rainstorm, and your tent is **un tent-able**, then you've got an **untenable** situation on your hands.

untoward (adjective): improper; troublesome. "un TOE ward"

Think: **undertow.**

The beach's dangerous **undertow** was **untoward**, dragging the girl underwater and loosening her bikini.

unwieldy (adjective): awkward; cumbersome. "un WEILD (rhymes with "field") y"

Think: **unable** to **wield.**

The ogre dropped his giant club and I picked it up, but it was too **unwieldy** to **wield** against him in battle.

upbraided (verb): criticized severely. "up BRAID ed"

Think: **upside braid.**

The hippie **upbraided** me so much that I was afraid she was going to slap me **upside** the head with her giant **braid**.

urbane (adjective): sophisticated; polite and polished. "ur BAIN"

Think: **urban**.

The farmboy moved to a hip **urban** city and became so **urbane** that he threw away his straw hat.

usurious (adjective): a rip-off. "you SIR y us"

Think: **u serious?**

I know that I have bad credit, but the **usurious** rate on my credit card made me say "**U serious?**"

usurp (verb): to illegally take by force. "ooh SURP"

Think: **u slurp**.

I know you're an anteater, but if you **usurp** my ant farm and **u slurp** up my ants, I'll be really angry.

utilitarian (adjective): useful. "you till-it TEAR y-en"

Think: **utilize**.

The military likes to buy **utilitarian** tools that can be **utilized** for many different tasks.

utopian (adjective): of a perfect society, ideal.
"you TOPE y-en"

Think: **You Tokin'**.

In an **utopian** world, you could be **tokin'** all the time, but that doesn't really work out in real life unless your name is Snoop Dog.

vacuous (adjective): stupid. "VACK you us"

Think: **vacuum**.

The beauty pageant contestant's answer was so **vacuous** that the judges thought her brain had been **vacuumed** out of her head.

vainglorious (adjective): boastful. "vane GLOR y us"

Think: **vain**.

The evil queen in <u>Snow White</u> is **vainglorious** - because she's **vain** and thinks she's **glorious**.

vanquished (adjective): defeated. "Van KWISHT"

Think: **van squished**.

If a **van squished** the ant crossing the road, then you could say that the ant has been **vanquished.**

vapid (adjective): dull; air-headed. "VAH pid"

Think: **vapor**.

All **vapor** and no substance, MTV is so **vapid** that it makes me want to take a nap.

variegated (adjective): varied.
"VAH ree GAIT (rhymes with "wait") ed"

Think: **varied**.

The autumn leaves in Vermont are known for their **variegated** colors; last year, they **varied** from red to yellow to orange.

vaunted (adjective): widely praised. "VON ted"

Think: **vaulted** well.

The gymnast **vaulted** so well that she was **vaunted** by the judges.

vehement (adjective): strongly emotional. "VE huh ment"

Think: **he meant it**.

His warning was so **vehement** that we knew **he meant it**.

venal (adjective): corrupt or corruptible. "VEE nil"

Think: **venereal** disease.

Nuns with **venereal** disease are, most likely, **venal**: they broke their oaths of chastity.

veracious (adjective): full of truth (veracity). "vur A shus"

Think: **verify**

If you can **verify** something, then it is **veracious** (truthful). (Not to be confused with "voracious")

verbose (adjective): wordy.
"vur BOES (rhymes with "toes")"

Think: **verb boss**.

They call me a **verb boss** since I am **verbose** and know a zillion different words.

verboten (adjective): forbidden. "fur BO tin"

Think: **verb eatin'**.

In North Korea, **verb eatin'** - instead of speaking one's mind - is common since many topics are **verboten**.

verisimilar (adjective): seeming to be true.
"VEH ree sim il er"

Think: **very similar**.

The conman's **verisimilar** story almost tricked me since it was **very similar** to the truth.

vernacular (noun): the way a certain group uses language.
"ver NACK u ler"

Think: **verb knack**.

Once you develop a **knack** for the way we use **verbs**, you'll have become familiar with our **vernacular**.

vertiginous (adjective): dizzy or producing dizziness.
"ver TIJ en is"

Think: **vertigo**.

Standing on the edge of the skyscraper made me feel really **vertiginous** because I have **vertigo**.

vestige (noun): last remains.
"VEST idge (rhymes with "fridge")"

Think: **vest**.

The explosion blew off most of my three-piece suit – the only **vestige** left was the **vest**.

vex (verb): to annoy. "VEKS"

Think: **hex**.

In *Harry Potter*, casting a **hex**, or spell designed to cause pain, on someone will definitely **vex** him.

vicarious (adjective): felt by imagining the experience of another. "vie CARE y us"

Think: **bi-curious**.

The **bi-curious** woman preferred to keep her fantasy **vicarious**, so she just watched.

vigilant (adjective): watchful; alert. "VIJ i lent"

Think: **vigilante**.

If you want some street justice, hire a **vigilante** - they are **vigilant** by nature.

vilify (verb): to speak ill of. "VILL if-i"

Think: **villain-fy**.

The dumpee decided to **vilify** her ex-boyfriend so the other girls would think he was a **villain**.

vindicate (verb): to prove correct; to free from blame. "VIN di kate"

Think: **Vin indicated**.

Judge **Vincent indicated** that the DNA evidence had fully **vindicated** the falsely accused defendant.

vindictive (adjective): wanting revenge. " vin DICT ive"

Think: **Vin Diesel**.

Vin Diesel often plays **vindictive** characters since he has been typecast as a tough guy.

virtuoso (noun): someone highly skilled at something. "vurr tyoo OH so"

Think: **virtues (oh so many)**.

Virtues? I have **oh so** many, because I'm a gosh-darned **virtuoso**.

virulent (adjective): infectious; harmful; hostile. "VIE roo lent"

Think: **virus**.

The swine flu **virus** is so **virulent** that it can kill a previously healthy person.

viscous (adjective): syrupy. "VISS kiss"

Think: **sticks to us**.

The **viscous Bisquick** pancake batter **sticks** to **us**.

vitiate (verb): to impair or degrade. "VIH she ate"

Think: **wish you ate**.

If you eat Taco Bell, it will **vitiate** your stomach and make you **wish you ate** something else.

vitriolic (adjective): full of hatred. "vit ri OL ic"

Think: **vitriolic alcoholic**.

Some people are just plain **mean** when they drink; there is nothing worse than a **vitriolic alcoholic**.

vituperated (verb): criticized harshly. "vie TOOP ur ated"

Think: **viper**.

He was **vituperated** so badly that he felt like he had been bitten by a **viper**.

vivacious (adjective): lively. "viv A shus"

Think: **Viva la Vida**.

The Coldplay song "**Viva la Vida**" means "long live life" and makes me want to be **vivacious**.

vocation (noun): job. "vo KAY shun"

Think: afford a **vacation**.

If you want to afford a **vacation** get a **vocation**.

vociferous (adjective): loud. "vo SIF er us"

Think: **voice for us**.

The announcer's loud **voice, for us**, was too **vociferous**.

volatile (adjective): unstable, dangerous. "VOL uh tull"

Think: **volcano isle**.

This may look like a peaceful island, but it's **volatile** – it's a **volcano isle** that could still erupt.

volition (noun): a conscious choice. "vo LISH un"

Think: **volunteer**.

No one forced him to **volunteer** for the mission; he did it of his own **volition**.

voluminous (adjective): large or numerous. "vo LUM in us"

Think: 18 **volume** diary.

I gave up on reading her diary after realizing how **voluminous** it was - it had 18 **volumes**!

voracious (adjective): having a huge appetite. "vo RAY shus"

Think: **carnivore ate us**.

The **carnivore ate us** because of its **voracious** appetite.

voyeur (noun): pervert, watcher, "Peeping Tom". "vo YER"

Think: **Foyer**.

Last night I caught a **voyeur** hanging out in the **foyer (entrance)** of my apartment building who was trying to spy into people's windows. Joke's on him: I was eating ice cream and wearing sweatpants.

waffle (verb): to go back and forth. "WAF ul"

Think: should I get **waffles**?

When I go out to brunch, I **waffle** (verb) between getting **waffles** (noun) and getting eggs.

wan (adjective): sick-looking. "WON"

Think: old Obi-**Wan**.

In <u>Star Wars</u>, Obi-**Wan** Kenobi looked **wan** even though he was a Jedi master because he was old.

wane (verb): to decrease in size, amount, length, or quantity. (rhymes with "pain")

Think: **Lil Wayne**.

The rapper **Lil Wayne** is only 5'5"; some might think his height has **waned**, but he has been that little since high school.

wanting (adjective): lacking or absent. " WONTING"

Think: **wanting** a boyfriend.

Wanting (verb) a boyfriend is normal if the romance in your life is **wanting** (adjective).

waspish (adjective): irritable. "WOSP ish"

Think: **wasp-ish**.

The trouble with keeping them as pets is that **wasps** are almost always **waspish** – they'll sting you if you look at them the wrong way.

watershed (noun): a turning point. "WAH ter shed"

Think: **Watergate**.

Nixon's involvement in the **Watergate** scandal was a **watershed** for his public opinion and led to his resignation.

wax (verb): to increase; to grow. "WAKS"

Think: ear **wax**.

Thanks to your body's glands, your sticky, orange-brown ear **wax** will **wax** daily even if you use Q-tips.

welter (verb): to be in turmoil; to get tossed around. "WEL turr"

Think: **welts**.

When I surf, I **welter** in the waves and my board hits me; I come out covered in **welts**.

whet (verb): to sharpen; to make more intense. "WET"

Think: **wet** mouth.

If you're starving and I show you a picture of a cheeseburger, it will **whet** your appetite and your mouth will water and get **wet**.

whimsical (adjective): playful; random; fanciful. "WIM sih kull"

Think: **whim**.

The princess's **whimsical** ideas included her sudden **whim** to travel to Antarctica.

willful (adjective): stubborn, insistent. "WILL full"

Think: **will-full**.

The **willful** horse was so **will-full** that he refused to be trained or ridden.

wily (adjective): clever; sly. "WHILE (rhymes with "trial") y"

Think: **Wile E.** Coyote.

Wile E. Coyote was not quite **wily** enough to catch the Roadrunner despite his clever traps.

winnow (verb): to separate the useful from the not-useful. "WIN no"

Think: **minnows**.

Winnow the **minnows** from your catch of fish; they're too small to eat.

winsome (adjective): charming and pleasing. "WIN sum"

Think: **win some** hearts.

She'll probably **win some** hearts at the dance due to her **winsome** manner.

wistful (adjective): sadly wishing for. "WIST ful"

Think: **wishful**.

The "Forever Alone" meme guy feels **wistful** because he is still alone after weeks of being **wishful** for a girlfriend.

wizened (adjective): shrunken and wrinkled, usually due to age. "WI zend"

Think: **wizard**.

Wizards like Gandalf and Dumbledore are usually **wizened** since they're really old.

wont (adjective): accustomed. "WONT"

Think: **want**.

It makes sense that you **want** to do things you are **wont** to doing, as opposed to trying risky new activities.

woo (verb): to seek or pursue romantically. "WOO"

Think: **woo-hoo!**

If you spend all night watching sports and exclaiming "**woo-hoo**!" then your chances of **wooing** your date drop dramatically.

workmanlike (adjective): good but not great. "WORK mun like"

Think: **workman's** design.

A **workman** will produce a **workmanlike** house design, but hire an architect if you want originality.

worldly (adjective): not spiritual; sophisticated; experienced. "WORLD lee"

Think: **world** traveler.

I've been all around the **world** and I, I, I, I can't find my baby (but I'm **worldly** now).

wrongheaded (adjective): having ideas that are wrong. "RONG head ed"

Think: **wrong foot**.

I think that we may have gotten off on the **wrong foot** when I made that **wrongheaded** remark about your fashion choices.

wry (adjective): cleverly and/or ironically humorous. "RYE"

Think: PB&J on **rye**.

Surprising me by serving a PB&J sandwich on **rye** bread is a good example of my mother's **wry** humor.

zealous (adjective): passionate. "ZELL us"

Think: **jealous**.

Zoe was so **zealous** about her first boyfriend that she became **jealous** of every other girl he knew.

zenith (noun): the highest point. "ZEE nith"

Think: **beneath**.

Once you reach the **zenith**, everything else is **beneath** it.

zephyr (noun): a gentle breeze. "ZEF ur"

Think: **zebra fur**.

The summer evening **zephyr** was as soft as **zebra fur**.

Appendix: Word Roots

Authors' Note: Word Roots are a helpful way to deduce the meaning of words that you don't know. They are not, however, foolproof: the English language is unpredictable, and full of words of which the standard meaning of the root is either flipped on its head (for example, the word "invaluable" means "valuable") or simply inaccurate. In other cases, the word root could have multiple languages of origin and thus the meaning of the word is unclear. This is why mnemonic devices are generally superior to word roots with regard to recalling the precise definition of a word. That being said, having incomplete information on a word is better than having none at all! We suggest that when creating your own mnemonics, you make sure to take special note whenever the word root goes against its most common interpretation.

a: without.

Think: **amoral** - without morality.

ab: away or apart from.

Think: **abnormal** - away from being normal.

ac: sharp; biting.

Think: **acid** - something that can chemically burn.

ad: toward or near.

Think: **adjacent** - next to.

ag: to do.

Think: **agent** - something that acts.

al: other.

Think: **alien** - something foreign.

am: love.

Think: **amour** - a love affair.

amb: to walk.

Think: **amble** - to walk slowly.

ambi: both.

Think: **ambidextrous** - able to use both hands.

anim: life.

Think: **animate** - to give life to.

ante: before.

Think: **antechamber** - the entryway before the main room.

anthro: human.

Think: **anthropology** - the study of man.

anti: against.

Think: **antifreeze** - chemical used against freezing.

apt: skill.

Think: **aptitude** - ability.

arch: the biggest.

Think: **archenemy** - the biggest enemy.

auto: self.

Think: **autonomy** - independence of the self.

be: to have.

Think: **befriend** - to become friends with.

bell: war.

Think: **belligerent** - warlike.

ben: good.

Think: **benefit** - an advantage.

bi: two.

Think: **bisexual** - having both male and female sexuality.

bon: good.

Think: **bonus**.

brev: short.

Think: **abbreviate** - to shorten.

cand: to burn.

Think: **candle**.

cap: head.

Think: **captain** - a leader.

card: heart.

Think: **cardiac** - of the heart.

carn: flesh.

Think: **carnivore** - a meat-eating animal.

chron: time.

Think: **chronology** - sequence of events.

circu: around.

Think: **circumference** - the distance around a circle.

cis: to cut.

Think: **scissors**.

clu: close.

Think: **conclusion**.

claim: to declare or shout.

Think: **exclaim** - to shout out.

cli: to lean.

Think: **recline** - to lean back.

col: together.

Think: **collaborate** - to work together.

con: together.

Think: **connect**.

cre: to grow.

Think: **increase**.

cred: to believe.

Think: **credibility** - believability.

cryp: hide.

Think: **cryptic** - having an unclear or hidden meaning.

culp: blame.

Think: **culprit** - one who is guilty.

de: reversal.

Think: **defame** - to take away the fame of (through slander).

dem: people.

Think: **democracy** - rule by the people.

dict: to say.

Think: **diction** - choice of words.

dign: worth.

Think: **dignity** - worthiness.

dis: reversal.

Think: **disarm** - to take away an **armament** (like a gun).

dac: to teach.

Think: **didactic** - intended to teach.

dog: belief.

Think: **dogma** - established beliefs.

dox: opinion.

Think: **orthodox** - adhering to established opinion.

dol: suffer.

Think: **condolences** - sympathy for another's suffering.

don: to give.

Think: **donate**.

dub: doubt.

Think: **dubious** - doubtful.

duct: to lead.

Think: orchestra **conductor**.

dur: hard.

Think: **durable**.

dys: faulty or broken.

Think: **dysfunctional**.

enni: year.

Think: **centennial** - a 100th anniversary.

epi: on.

Think: **epidermis** - the layer of the skin on the dermis.

equ: equal.

Think: **equal**.

err: to wander.

Think: **error**.

eu: good.

Think: **eulogy** - a praising speech.

ex: out

Think: **exclude**.

extra: outside of.

Think: **extraterrestrial** - outside of Earth.

fac: to make.

Think: **factory**.

fer: to bring.

Think: **transfer**.

ferv: to burn.

Think: **fervor** - passion.

fid: faith.

Think: **fidelity** - faithfulness.

fin: end.

Think: **final**.

flam: to burn.

Think: **flame**.

flex: to bend.

Think: **flexible**.

flict: to hit.

Think: **conflict** - fighting.

flu: to flow.

Think: **fluid**.

fore: before.

Think: **foreshadow** - to hint at the future.

fort: chance.

Think: **fortune**-teller.

frac: to break.

Think: **fracture**.

found: bottom.

Think: **foundation**.

fus: to pour.

Think: blood **transfusion** - transferring blood into someone.

362

gen: type.

Think: **gender** - sex.

gn: know.

Think: **recognize**.

grand: large.

Think: **Grand** Canyon.

grat: pleasing.

Think: **grateful**.

grav: heavy.

Think: **gravity**.

greg: group.

Think: **congregrate** - to group together.

hes: to stick.

Think: **adhesive**.

hetero: different.

Think: **heterosexual** - sexual with a sex different than one's own.

hom: same.

Think: **homosexual** - sexual with one's own sex.

hyper: over.

Think: A **hyperactive** little kid.

hypo: under.

Think: **hypothermia** – body temperature below normal.

im: not.

Think: **impossible**.

in: not.

Think: **insane**.

inter: between.

Think: **interstate** highway.

364

intra: within.

Think: **intravenous** - within a vein.

ject: to throw.

Think: **eject**.

junct: to join.

Think: **junction**.

lect: to choose.

Think: **elect**.

lev: lift.

Think: **elevator**.

log: speech.

Think: **dialogue**.

lum: light.

Think: **illuminate**.

mag: big.

Think: **magnify**.

mal: bad.

Think: **malicious**.

man: hand.

Think: **manual** labor.

min: small.

Think: **minimum**.

mit: to send.

Think: **transmit**.

misc: mixed.

Think: **miscellaneous**.

morph: shape.

Think: **amorphous** - without shape.

mort: death.

Think: **immortal** - without death.

mut: change.

Think: **mutate**.

nox: harm.

Think: **obnoxious**.

nym: name.

Think: **synonym**.

nov: new.

Think: **novice** - a beginner.

omni: all.

Think: **omnipotent** - all powerful.

pac: peace.

Think: **pacifier**.

pan: all.

Think: **panoramic** - taking in all the scenery.

par: equal.

Think: **disparity** - difference.

para: next to.

Think: **parallel**.

path: feeling.

Think: **empathy**.

ped: child.

Think: **pediatrician** - child doctor.

ped: foot.

Think: **pedal**.

pen: to pay.

Think: **compensation** - payment.

pend: to hang.

Think: **pendulum**.

peri: around.

Think: **perimeter**.

pet: to strive.

Think: **compete**.

phil: love.

Think: **bibliophile** - one who loves books.

phone: sound.

Think: **megaphone**.

plac: to please.

Think: **placate** - to calm down or appease.

ple: to fill.

Think: **complete**.

pos: to place.

Think: **deposit**.

port: to carry.

Think: **import**.

post: after.

Think: **posthumous** - after death.

pov: poor.

Think: **poverty**.

pre: before.

Think: **preview**.

prehend: to get.

Think: **comprehend**.

pro: a lot.

Think: **profuse** - large in quantity.

370

prob: to test.

Think: **probe**.

pug: to fight.

Think: **pugilist** - a boxer.

punct: to prick.

Think: **puncture**.

quis: to search for.

Think: **inquisitive** - seeking knowledge.

qui: quiet.

Think: **quiet**.

rid: to laugh.

Think: **ridicule**.

rog: to ask.

Think: **interrogate** - to question intensely.

sacr: holy.

Think: **sacred**.

sci: to know.

Think: **conscious**.

scribe: to write.

Think: **scribble**.

se: apart.

Think: **separate**.

seq: to follow.

Think: **sequence**.

sens: to be aware.

Think: **sense**.

sol: to loosen.

Think: **dissolve**.

spec: to look.

Think: **spectator**.

sta: to be still.

Think: **static** - still.

sua: smooth.

Think: **suave**.

sub: below.

Think: **submarine**.

super: above.

Think: **supersonic** - faster than sound.

tac: silent.

Think: **tacit** - understood without words.

tain: to hold.

Think: **contain**.

tens: to stretch.

Think: **tension**.

theo: God.

Think: **atheist** - without belief in God.

tort: to twist.

Think: **contort** - to bend severely.

tract: to pull.

Think: **attract**.

trans: across.

Think: **transport**.

ut: to use.

Think: **utensil**.

ver: truth.

Think: **verify**.

374

vi: life.

Think: **viable** - able to survive.

vid: to see.

Think: **video**.

vok: to call.

Think: **invoke** - to summon.

vol: to wish.

Think: **voluntary** - of one's own wish.

Index of Words

analogue

anathema

anile

animosity

annotation

annul

anodyne

anomaly

antedate

antediluvian

antipode

antithesis

apace

apartheid

aplomb

apocryphal

apoplectic

apostle

apothegm

apotheosis

appease

apportion

apposite

approbation

apropos

arbitrary

arcane

arch

archaic

arduous

arid

arrogate

articulate

artifice

artless

ascendancy

ascetic

ashen

askew

asperity

aspersion

aspiration

assail

assiduous

assuage

astray

astute

attenuate

audacious

augment

august

auspicious

austere

authoritative

automaton

autonomous

avaricious

aver

aversion

avuncular

badger

baleful

banal

base

battery

bauble

baying

beatific

beatify
becalm
bedlam
beguile
behemoth
beleaguered
belied
belittle
bellicose
bemoan
beneficence
benign
bereft
beseech
bifurcated
bilious
blasé
blithe
bloviated
bludgeon
bonhomie
boon
boor
bootless
bowdlerize
bravado
brazen
brevity
bromide
brusque
bucolic
bugbear
bulwark
bumptious

bungle
buoyant
burdensome
burgeoning
buttress
bygone
byzantine
cache
cacophony
cadge
cajole
calamitous
callous
callow
calumnious
camaraderie
canard
canny
canonize
capacious
capitulate
capricious
captious
cardinal
caricatured
castigate
caterwaul
causal
celerity
censure
cerebral
chagrin
champion
chary

chicanery
choleric
chronological
churlish
cinematic
circuitous
circumscribed
circumspect
circumvents
clairvoyant
clandestine
clangorous
clemency
climatic
climax
cloying
coalesce
cocksure
coddle
coerced
coeval
cognizant
coherence
cohesive
cohort
coin
collusion
commensurate
commiserate
companionable
complicit
composure
compunction
concession

concoct
concomitant
concord
concupiscence
condign
condones
conferred
confiscate
conflagration
conflate
confound
conglomerate
conniving
connoisseur
conscientious
conspicuous
consternation
contumacious
conundrum
conversant
copious
cordial
cordon
corroborate
cosmopolitan
covert
cowed
craven
credence
credulous
crepuscular
crestfallen
cryptic
cull

culminate
culpable
cumbersome
cunning
cupidity
curmudgeon
cursory
curtail
cynical
cynosure
daunt
dearth
debacle
debased
debauchery
debilitate
decadent
decimate
declaimed
decorous
decrepit
decried
defamatory
defenestrate
defunct
degenerate
delectable
deleterious
delimit
delineate
demagogue
demarcate
demean
demeanor

demotic
demur
denigrate
denizen
denuded
depiction
deplete
deplore
depredate
deride
derivative
descry
desecrate
desiccated
despoiled
despot
desuetude
deteriorate
devoid
devolve
devout
dexterity
diabolical
diaphanous
diatribe
dichotomy
didactic
diffident
digression
dilatory
dilettante
dilute
dint
dire

discomfit
disconcert
discreet
discrepancy
discrete
discriminate
disgruntled
dismantle
dismissive
disparage
disparate
dispassionate
dispatch
displacing
disputatious
dissemble
disseminated
distension
dither
diurnal
divergent
divisive
docile
doctrinaire
doggedness
doggerel
dogmatic
dolorous
dormant
dour
draconian
droll
dubious
dudgeon

dupe
duplicitous
dwindle
dyspeptic
ebullient
eclectic
effaced
effete
efficacious
efflorescence
effluvium
effrontery
effusive
egalitarian
egregious
eldritch
emancipate
embellish
embroiled
embryonic
eminent
emollient
emphatic
empirical
encomium
encompass
encroaching
enervating
enigmatic
enmity
ennui
ensorcelled
entitled
entreat

ephemeral
epitome
equivocal
eradicate
ersatz
erstwhile
erudite
eschew
esoteric
espouse
espy
estimable
estranged
ethereal
etiolated
euphemism
eurytopic
evanescent
evinced
exacerbated
exact
exacting
exaggerate
excise
excoriated
exculpated
execrable
exigent
exodus
exorbitant
expatiate
expatriate
expedient
explicate

exponent
expunge
expurgate
extant
extemporaneous
extenuating
extirpate
extol
extraneous
extrapolate
exult
fabricate
facetious
fallible
fanatic
farce
fastidious
fatuous
fawning
feckless
fecund
feign
felicity
ferret
fervor
festoon
fetid
fiasco
filial
fillip
finagled
finicky
fitful
flagrant

fleeting
flippant
florid
flotilla
flotsam
flounder
flourish
flouted
fluctuate
flummoxed
foible
foment
forage
forbearance
foreground
forestall
formidable
fortitude
fortuitous
fracas
fractious
fraternize
frenetic
froward
frugal
fruition
fudge
fuliginous
fulsome
funereal
furor
furtive
gadfly
gaffe

gainsay
gallant
gambit
gamboled
garble
gargantuan
garrulous
gauche
gaudy
genial
germane
germinate
ghastly
gild
glacial
glancing
glaring
glowered
glut
goosebumps
gossamer
grandiloquent
grandiose
grandstand
grasping
grating
gravitas
gregarious
grisly
grouse
grovel
gumption
guttural
hackneyed

haggard
halcyon
hallowed
hapless
haptic
harangue
harbinger
hardscrabble
harmonious
harried
harrow
haughty
headlong
hector
hegemony
heinous
herald
hermetic
heterodox
heterogeneous
heyday
hiatus
hidebound
hirsute
histrionic
hodgepodge
holistic
homespun
homogeneous
hortatory
hubris
humbuggery
humdrum
husbandry

iconoclast
ideological
idyllic
idiosyncrasy
ignominy
illiberal
illusory
imbroglio
imminent
immure
immutable
impassive
impeccable
impecunious
impeded
impenetrable
imperative
imperious
imperturbable
impetuous
impetus
impinge
implacable
implication
implicit
imploring
importune
impregnable
imprimatur
impromptu
impudence
impugn
inalienable
inane

incandescent
incensed
inchoate
incipient
incisive
incoherent
incorporate
incorrigible
inculcate
incumbent
indefatigable
indictment
indigenous
indignant
indomitable
industrious
ineffable
ineluctable
inestimable
inexorable
infinitesimal
influx
ingenious
ingenuous
ingrained
ingratiate
inimical
inimitable
innate
innocuous
inordinate
inscrutable
insinuate
insipid

insolence
insular
integrate
interloper
intimate
intrepid
intrinsic
intrusive
inundated
inveigh
inveigle
invidious
inviolate
irascible
irk
ironic
irresolute
jargon
jejune
jettison
jingoism
jocose
judicious
juggernaut
juvenescence
juxtapose
kindle
kindred
kismet
kowtow
lachrymose
lackadaisical
laconic
lampoon

languid
largess
lassitude
latent
laudable
lax
legerdemain
lenient
levity
licentious
lionized
listless
logorrhea
loquacious
lovelorn
lucid
lucre
ludicrous
lugubrious
lumber
luminary
lurid
macabre
macerate
machination
maelstrom
magisterial
magnanimous
magnate
makeshift
malevolent
malfeasance
malign
malinger

malleable
manacle
mandate
manifold
marginal
marshal
maudlin
mawkish
meager
meddle
meld
mellifluous
melodramatic
mendacity
mendicant
menial
mephitic
mercenary
mercurial
meretricious
meterological
meticulous
mettle
miasma
microcosm
milieu
milquetoast
mimetic
minatory
minion
misanthrope
miscreant
miserly
misnomer

mitigate
modicum
modish
monastic
morass
morbid
mordant
mores
moribund
morose
motile
motley
multifaceted
mundane
munificent
myopic
myriad
nadir
naivete
nascent
nebulous
neophyte
nepotism
nettle
newfangled
noisome
non sequitur
nonchalant
nondescript
nonpareil
nonplussed
nontrivial
normative
nostalgia

nostrum
notorious
novel
novitiate
noxious
nuance
nugatory
obdurate
obeisance
obfuscated
objectionable
objective
objurgation
obloquy
obsequious
obstinate
obstreperous
obtrusive
occluded
odious
officious
offset
ogle
omission
omniscient
onus
opaque
openhanded
opine
opportune
opprobrium
opulent
ornate
orthodox

oscillate
ossified
ostentatious
ostracized
otiose
outmoded
outstrip
overshadow
overweening
pacific
painstaking
palatable
palatial
palimpsest
pall
palliate
pallid
panacea
pander
pangs
panned
paradigm
paragon
pariah
parley
parochial
parody
paroxysm
parsimonious
partiality
partisan
pastiche
pathos
patois

paucity
pedantic
pedestrian
peevish
penchant
pendulous
penitent
penurious
penury
peons
peregrinate
peremptory
perennial
perfidy
perfunctory
peripatetic
peripheral
permeated
permutation
pernicious
perquisites
personified
perspicacious
pertinacious
perturb
pervasive
perverse
petulant
philander
phlegmatic
physiological
picaresque
picayune
picturesque

piebald
pilfer
pillory
pinnacle
pioneering
piquant
pitfall
pith
pittance
pivotal
placate
plaintive
platitude
platonic
plaudits
plausible
plebeian
plenipotentiary
pluck
plutocracy
polarize
polemic
politesse
politic
pomp
ponderous
portentous
poseur
posit
posthumous
pragmatic
prattle
precarious
precocious

precursor
predilection
premonition
prescient
pretext
prevarication
primed
primordial
pristine
proclivity
prodigal
prodigious
profane
profligacy
profound
profuse
progenitors
prognosticate
proliferate
prolific
prolix
prominent
promulgate
pronounced
propagate
propensity
prophetic
propitious
propriety
prosaic
protean
providential
provincial
prowess

proximity
prudent
puerile
pugnacious
pulchritude
punctilious
pungent
punitive
purist
pusillanimous
putrid
quagmire
quail
quandary
quash
querulous
quiescent
quintessential
quixotic
quizzical
quotidian
raconteur
ragamuffin
raiment
ramification
rampant
rancorous
rankled
rapacious
rapt
rapturous
rarefied
rash
raucous

raze
readily
realization
reap
rebuttal
recalcitrant
recant
recapitulated
recidivist
reclusive
recondite
recrudescent
rectitude
redouble
redress
reductive
redundant
refracted
refractory
refulgent
refute
rejuvenated
relinquish
relish
remedial
reminiscent
remiss
remunerated
renowned
repertoire
replete
reprehensible
reprobate
reprove

repudiate
repugnant
requisite
resigned
resilient
resolute
resonant
respite
resplendent
restitution
restive
resurgence
reticent
retiring
retrenchment
retrospection
revamp
revanche
reverberate
reverent
revile
revulsion
rhapsodize
rhetorical
rickety
rift
riposte
risible
risque
roborant
robust
rotund
row
rudimentary

ruffian
ruminate
saccharine
sacrosanct
salacious
salient
salubrious
salutary
sangfroid
sanguine
sap
sapid
sapient
sardonic
sashayed
satiated
scanty
scapegoat
scathing
schadenfreude
schism
scintillating
sclerotic
scofflaw
scotch
scrupulous
scrutinize
scuffle
scurrilous
scuttle
secretes
sectarian
secular
sedentary

sedulous

segue

self-styled

semblance

seminal

sententious

sentient

sequacious

sere

serendipity

servile

sham

shard

shelve

shirk

showy

shrewd

simper

simulacrum

sinuous

skittish

skulduggery

skulk

slake

slander

slatternly

slipshod

slothful

slovenly

sojourn

solecism

solicitous

solidarity

solipsistic

somnolent

sonorous

sophistry

sophomoric

soporific

sordid

soupcon

sovereign

sparing

sparse

specious

spendthrift

splenetic

spurious

squalid

squelch

stalwart

stanch

staple

statuesque

staunch

steadfast

stigmas

stilted

stolid

storied

stratagem

streamlined

strenuous

stricture

strident

stringent

stultify

stupefied

subjective
sublime
subsequent
subsidy
substantiate
subversive
subvert
succor
succumb
sullen
sumptuary
superficial
supplant
surly
surmise
surpassing
surreptitious
susceptible
swathe
sybarite
sycophant
synergy
synoptic
syntax
taciturn
tangible
taxonomic
temerity
temperance
tempestuous
temporal
tenable
tendentious
tensile

tenuous
tepid
terse
timorous
tirade
titular
tonic
toothsome
torpid
tortuous
totalitarian
touted
tranquil
transgression
transitory
treacly
tremulous
trepidation
trifling
truculent
truncated
tumid
tumultuous
turbid
turgid
turpitude
ubiquitous
umbrage
unadorned
unassuming
unbridled
unconscionable
unconventional
unctuous

uncultivated
undermine
underscore
understated
undulate
uniform
unkempt
unpretentiousness
unpropitious
unruly
unsavory
untenable
untoward
unwieldy
upbraided
urbane
usurious
usurp
utilitarian
utopian
vacuous
vainglorious
vanquished
vapid
variegated
vaunted
vehement
venal
veracious
verbose
verboten
verisimilar
vernacular
vertiginous

vestige
vex
vicarious
vigilant
vilify
vindicate
vindictive
virtuoso
virulent
viscous
vitiate
vitriolic
vituperated
vivacious
vocation
vociferous
volatile
volition
voluminous
voracious
voyeur
waffle
wan
wane
wanting
waspish
watershed
wax
welter
whet
whimsical
willful
wily
winnow

winsome

wistful

wizened

wont

woo

workmanlike

worldly

wrongheaded

wry

zealous

zenith

zephyr

Acknowledgments

We mainly used the online version of the Merriam-Webster dictionary (www.m-w.com) for definitions. We'd like to thank Edwin Kotchian for his editing, feedback, and creative suggestions.

Made in the USA
Middletown, DE
27 June 2023

33953503R00219